The One of a Kind Financial Plan™

Say Goodbye to One Size Fits All and
Hello to What Actually Works

MIKE MILLIGAN

The One of a Kind Financial Plan™

Say Goodbye to One Size Fits All and Hello to What Actually Works

Design and cover art by Peaceful Profits.

Paperback ISBN: 978-1-967587-02-5
eBook ISBN: 978-1-967587-07-0

I dedicate this book to Jonathan,
my brother.
He lived a One-of-a-Kind Life.

CONTENTS

INTRODUCTION

If you've ever felt fed up with the financial industry, you're not alone. As someone who's been working in it for 26 years, I can tell you that the industry is a setup. Not an intentional one—not some grand conspiracy—but a setup, nonetheless.

The financial industry is unapproachable, overly serious, and burdened by heavy regulations. But the **real problem** isn't just that the industry is overly complex—or even the regulations. It's that it's *one size fits all*. The system is designed to be repeatable. Why? So financial companies can make a profit.

If companies can replicate the process and sell you on the idea, then rinse and repeat, they benefit. It's efficient. It's smart. But it's not right. The truth is that the financial industry is selling an idea. Their prevailing message is: do XYZ, and you'll achieve financial success. It's like Retirement Déjà Vu every time I speak with an individual working with a large firm and the plan they proposed.

But life isn't a formula, and financial plans shouldn't be either. A cookie-cutter approach will never be as powerful as creating a unique plan tailored to your needs. You can't change the financial industry on a broad scale. But that doesn't mean you have to accept it. You can change the way you approach your finances individually by taking control and building something that truly works for you.

Through the pages of this book, the #1 thing I want you to understand is that you live a one-of-a-kind life. Everyone does. As Steve Jobs put it, "Your time is limited, so don't waste it living someone else's life."[1] There is nobody else on this planet who is living the same life as you. And so for that reason, your financial plan shouldn't be created without *you* and your one-of-a-kind life in mind.

You might feel like you've been pigeonholed into certain financial choices or constrained by what society or the industry says you "should" do. But it doesn't have to be that way. You can design a financial plan that addresses your individual hurdles and helps you achieve financial independence, security, generational wealth, a comfortable retirement—and more importantly, a plan that makes the one-of-a-kind life that you want to live a reality.

In 1997, Apple made waves with the slogan "Think Differently." And even the staunchest Android users have to admit that Apple changed the game, creating possibilities that few ever imagined. (Remember BlackBerry and Nokia? I'm sure they would emphatically say the game changed and they didn't—that's why they're no longer around or meaningful.)

Over the course of my career, I've worked to think differently about money. I've helped countless clients navigate their financial journeys and live the lives of their dreams. I've grown a nationwide team that attracts clients from all over the country who are looking for a different type

---

1 Stanford News, "'You've Got to Find What You Love,' Jobs Says," *Stanford News*, June 14, 2005, https://news.stanford.edu/stories/2005/06/youve-got-find-love-jobs-says.

of financial planner. I've even been brought into universities to lecture, teaching future financial professionals that there is more to financial planning than offering one-size-fits-all advice.

My approach isn't a game changer because I'm smarter or better than anyone else or because I have some hidden tech that nobody else has. It works because I start at a different place: with **you.**

This book exists to teach you that approach and to show you how to create a financial plan as unique as your life.

If you're reading this book for yourself, my ultimate goal is to teach you how to think differently about your finances. **You don't need one-size-fits-all advice—you need a One of a Kind Financial Plan™ that helps you build a one-of-a-kind life.**

And if you're a financial professional reading this book, in these pages you will discover a different, *better* way to serve your clients—one built on their individuality.

HOW TO READ THIS BOOK

This book is divided into three parts, each one building on the other to help you think differently about your life, your money, and how to create your future.

In Part 1, I'll share my personal journey in the financial industry and stories from clients who have used one-of-a-kind plans to create lives that light them up. Even though everyone's path is different, you'll see that there are universal principles that can guide you. In these chapters, you'll learn:

- Why the traditional financial industry offers a one-size-fits-all approach (and why that isn't what you need).
- The #1 step you can take to make a significant impact on your financial future.
- How you can start creating a financial plan that is built for you and the life you want NOW, without a significant time investment.

In Part 2, we'll dive into the practical steps needed to create a customized financial plan. I'll outline my system, the **One of a Kind Financial Plan**™. It's a five-step process that allows you to make strategic financial choices, create both security and growth, rest assured that you won't run out of money in retirement, and live your dream life now and in the future.

Finally, Part 3 is all about action. We'll take everything you've learned and apply it to your specific situation. You'll:

- Define what your one-of-a-kind life looks like
- Discover how to create YOUR One of a Kind Financial Plan™
- Learn how to build the knowledge and the team to support you along the way

If that all sounds overwhelming, know that everything boils down to three main points:

Point #1: Everyone deserves a one-of-a-kind life—a life that not only fulfills you now but leaves a legacy that inspires others to carve out their own unique paths.

Point #2: One-of-a-kind lives don't happen by accident. You can't stumble into them. Along with a vision for living, you need a One of a Kind Financial Plan™ that helps you get there.

Point #3: Creating that plan is not an impossible task. You *can* learn what it takes, and you can start today—no matter where you've come from or what mistakes you've made along the way.

By the end of this book, you'll have a clear roadmap to your one-of-a-kind life, along with the tools and confidence to make it a reality.

This book is here to remind you that your life is unique. It's unlike anyone else's—and it requires an individualized approach.

It's time to think differently about your money.

If, as you read this book, you have any questions about how to put what you learn into action, or if you feel like you are ready for professional support with your One of a Kind Financial Plan™, you can book a call with me or a member of my nationwide team at www.mikemilligan.com.

Let's get started,
Mike Milligan

—Be One of a Kind

PART 1

This Is Personal

CHAPTER 1

WHERE ARE YOU HEADING?

I recently met with a man who had done quite well for himself financially—at 47 years old, he had a substantial net worth.

"I've met my goal," he told me. "$5 million."

He might have expected me to be impressed, to congratulate him, or to assure him that he had done everything "right" and that his financial plan was right where it needed to be. Instead, I asked him a question that stopped him in his tracks.

"Now what?"

He stared at me blankly at first. He had come to me just to make sure he didn't make any mistakes as he continued to grow his money. But he hadn't expected me to ask *that*.

"I…don't know," he admitted. "Nobody's ever asked me that before."

I tried to help him along. "Do you want to travel? Do you want to spend more time with your wife? Start a charity? Do something you've never done before? What is it that you want from this life?"

The sad part is, he couldn't answer. Every step he had taken on his financial path, every money decision he'd made, everything he'd saved and invested and strategized— he had no idea *why* he was even doing it.

"Until you can answer these questions, I can't really do anything for you," I finally told him.

He was shocked. I have no doubt that he'd connected with other professionals in the financial industry over the years. I'm sure he got a lot of well-meaning guidance. And it seems like some of the advice, on the surface, paid off.

But he was falling into the trap that so many people fall into. He was trying to buy happiness without ever considering what it is that would really make him happy.

Now, that's not to say that I fully buy into the old adage "money doesn't buy you happiness." Like most advice passed down generation to generation, there's definitely truth to it.

Most of us know by now that happiness isn't based on the number in our financial accounts, but by whatever it is that we love the most. For some of us, that's family. For some, it's adventure, travel, or novelty. For others, it's making a difference in the world.

But I also know two things. The first is that every single one of you out there is living a *one-of-a-kind life*. It doesn't matter if you're traveling the world as a digital nomad or spending your days at a corporate 9–5. Your life is different from everyone else's life—and the life you *want* isn't like anyone else's either.

The second is that when you have more money, it allows you to spend more time on the things you love and with the people you love. In other words, having money helps you live *your one-of-a-kind life*—the life that brings you passion, fulfillment, and happiness.

> *Having money helps you live your one-of-a-kind life—the life that brings you passion, fulfillment, and happiness.*

But here's the catch—because that life is unique, the path you need to take with your money is also unique.

We're not put on this earth to follow a straight line, living life just like everyone else around us. In fact, when we are kids, our parents go out of their way to tell us how special and unique we are. They encourage us to try things, to be ourselves, to be unique individuals.

But somewhere along the line, the world stops encouraging us to do things our own way. Corporations and companies—and even schools, for that matter—put us on an assembly line. Go to school. Study. Get good grades. Graduate. Get a job. Toe the line. Spend 50 years working to make money for someone else. Then, hopefully, retire—and maybe finally get to do what we want. We're trained out of our uniqueness. We're trained out of reaching for what we want. And we're trained out of thinking differently.

So many of us spend our whole lives pigeonholed into what we think we're "supposed" to do. And the financial industry is no exception.

In the first decade of my career, I worked in regional banking and insurance. I'd gone to school to learn the knowledge I needed. But it wasn't until I started working that I *really* got an education.

I saw clients who had done all the "right" things and followed the advice that seemed great on paper. But when the stock market, which was supposed to go up 8–10% every year, didn't do that, they were left without an answer. The value of the stock market in 2000 and the value of the stock market in 2013 were exactly the same. Instead of people's nest eggs growing the way they had been told they would, their assets were actually losing value—the market was going down, as they were retiring and pulling their money out.

When I saw the struggles that people were going through and the barriers they were facing because they hadn't been taught how to financially plan, I knew that something wasn't right. There had to be a different way to set people up, where they could be protected, grow their money, do something other than check off boxes that didn't pay off for them in the end. I looked around me and identified the assembly line people were on, and I realized I wanted to be different.

But looking back, I realized that the seeds for me to think differently were planted long before I entered the industry.

I grew up in a very small town in North Carolina. My family was dirt poor—my grandparents lived in a single-wide mobile home. But we were lucky because we had each other. Every Sunday, we gathered together for a family meal.

When I was 11 years old, my granny, Elizabeth, at age 64, decided that she was going to take a family recipe that had been passed down from generation to generation and use it to add some money to the family. She started making collard sandwiches in bulk to sell.

She sold her sandwiches at festivals and in convenience

stores. People would line up at her trailer every day to buy them for lunch. Soon she started adding some of her delicious desserts, including her town-famous, 14-layer chocolate cakes.

This wasn't something any other grandmothers, who I knew, were doing. But it's a good thing she did. Just a couple of years later, everything changed for her and everyone in my family. My grandfather, Walter, was diagnosed with cancer. It was an aggressive form, one that took him within six months.

I was crushed. He and my granny were two of my "Mount Rushmore people" who stood large and inspired me throughout the course of my life. My granny had lost the love of her life—they'd been together 50 years. But she didn't wallow in her loss because she knew she had to lead our family. My grandfather's income was gone, and she had to take care of everyone.

She pulled me into her sandwich business. I would deliver sandwiches, help her negotiate with customers, and then count money at her dining room table after school. All of our other family members were there too, along for the ride, coming together to make this happen—because that's what families do.

And years later, when I was working in the financial industry, looking around and knowing that I had to do things a different way, I asked myself, *where did I learn this? How did I know to look at things differently?* The answer lay back there at that dining room table, watching my grandmother make decisions that were out of the ordinary so she could take care of everyone.

Our family gathered and worked together to help my granny deliver sandwiches, watching her step into her own power to support us. A traditional one-size-fits-all financial plan never could have captured those moments.

After my grandfather's death, my family had to change. We had to look at money differently—and to do what it took to survive in a different way.

That's where I started to learn the value of a One of a Kind Financial Plan™. But the problem is that most of us aren't taught to think about money in this way. We're put on that same assembly line of life that everyone else is on, and we're told that everything will be fine. But we're not told to think about where it is that we're trying to get to in the first place to create the life we want to live.

We think we're doing what we're supposed to be doing. We work hard. We save. We trust Wall Street advisors.

But there's a big difference between saving for the future and *investing for the future*. There's a difference between moving money into a bank account and using your money to create a multiplication effect. This means to exponentially grow that money so that you can reach your financial goals sooner and live the life you want without waiting until it's too late.

That's what I have taught countless clients to do. I'm going to share some powerful case studies that will show you what happens when you build the knowledge, the vision, and the plan you need to get the life you truly want:

Case Study #1: Richard, Donna, and Connie

(Note that the names of all clients throughout this book have been changed to protect their privacy.)

On the outside, Richard and Donna might look like people who were all set, who just needed to follow that one-size-fits-all approach.

They had money and success. Donna was a corporate career woman—a very big deal. She was an executive for a Fortune 500 company.

I could have given them very traditional advice, setting them up for a linear retirement path. But that's not what they *really needed*.

You see, Richard and Donna had a 20-year age gap. She knew the day she married him that there would come a time when she would become not just his wife but his caregiver.

And we needed to plan for *that*. We needed to set her up to retire early enough with enough money to provide not just for herself but to care for Richard.

That's exactly what we did. We planned for long-term expenses. We ensured that Richard and Donna's money would fund the future they wanted. And we paved the way for them to travel and soak up as much life together as they possibly could before he reached an age where he needed her to step into that caregiver role. In fact, they recently went to Hawaii together, resting easily knowing that their financial plan is secured and their future is laid out for them. Donna is so grateful for the time they have spent together and the adventures they've had supported by their financial plan.

As she looks to the future they've laid out for themselves, she is ready to welcome a new phase, and is happy to care for her husband. She's even moved her mom in to become a caregiver for her as well. She's been able to live one phase of her one-of-a-kind life and is looking forward to the next.

This isn't the life everyone would want—but it's *her* one-of-a-kind life. Donna recently told me that she already has plans for what comes later down the line as well. When Richard passes away and she enters into her next chapter, she and a group of her girlfriends plan to purchase property and live together, Golden Girls style, living out the end of their lives supporting each other every step of the way.

Donna and Richard are a tale of success. But there's a third party in their story. For years, I met with Donna in her office. We talked about the future, what it would look like, what she needed to prepare for, and the path to get her there. We talked about how to mitigate her taxes and free up her income so that she could invest strategically and retire earlier, maximizing her time with Richard and ultimately stepping into the role she knew was coming.

What I didn't know was that I wasn't just educating Donna. Donna had an assistant, Connie. And she sat in on these meetings, taking notes for Donna.

One day, Connie pulled me aside as I was about to leave and asked if she could set up a meeting with me.

I gladly took the meeting, assuming that Connie would be working with a much more limited income than Donna and Richard's. So when she told me she had saved $1.2 million, I was floored! I almost didn't believe her.

"How could you have saved this on an assistant's salary?" I asked her.

She looked at me and said, "Because everything you ever told Donna to do, I did too."

I was so impressed by Connie's boldness, her ability to learn, and what she had accomplished. And when I started asking her questions to help her visualize her one-of-a-kind life, it became apparent that, unlike Donna, what she needed was the freedom to retire, as early as possible.

Connie had spent years working hard for someone else—Donna—someone she cared about deeply, but it was hard work nonetheless. And she was ready to *live* in a way that she hadn't been able to up to this point. She wanted to enjoy her life on her own terms.

We set her up to retire at age 50. When she retired, Connie played golf, traveled, and thrived in her retirement life with joy and wonder. And at 56, she was diagnosed with cancer. She died two years later.

Here's Connie's lesson to all of us. She had no way of knowing that when she retired, she only had eight years to live. But her one-of-a-kind plan gave her eight years of freedom and fulfillment that she wouldn't have had otherwise. It saved her from living a life for others until the day she died. She spent those last years living life on her terms—and I am humbled that I was able to contribute to make this possible for her.

Case Study #2: Ben

Ben was a federal employee who had worked hard and had done what he was "supposed" to do for his entire life. But Ben had a passion: He loved to ride Harley-Davidsons.

When I first started working with Ben, I encouraged him to visualize what he wanted to spend his days doing—what made him unique—and how he wanted his money to work for him in retirement.

Part of him might have felt a little silly explaining to me

that what he really wanted to do with his retirement was to ride motorcycles. But as soon as I heard him talking about it, I could tell that this was his one-of-a-kind life. It lit him up. He had a sparkle in his eye like a kid on Christmas morning. I knew we would create a plan that allowed him to spend as much time as possible riding.

We had a lot of work to do. Like so many people I meet, Ben had never been given strong, solid financial planning advice that made it possible for him to grow his money to its full potential.

I helped him understand how to allocate his assets strategically, mitigate his taxes, invest effectively, plan for his long-term care, and to make sure his family was cared for. Most importantly, I taught him how to put his money to work to create the future he wanted.

And sure enough, that's what Ben did when he retired— he put his one-of-a-kind plan into play to create his one-of-a-kind life. A couple of years ago, Ben had a motorcycle accident…and his perspective on life completely changed. He will never be able to ride a motorcycle again. But he recently told me that due to his accident, and the way he chose to spend his time now that he can no longer ride, he is closer to his family than he ever could have imagined. And he would not change a thing.

Ben's life, as life will do, took a turn that led him along a winding path. But the work we put into his one-of-a-kind plan allowed him to live his passion for as long as he could, and to connect with his other passion, his family, in a whole new way.

Case Study #3: My Brother, Jonathan

This case study is near and dear to my heart—not only because he was my brother, not only because I loved him, but because this experience solidified for me how important my work is, and how vital it is that I commit to my *own* one-of-a-kind life.

My brother, Jonathan, was always the complete opposite of me. I was straitlaced, buttoned up. I played sports. I was academic. I knew I wanted to go to college. Jonathan was country. He liked riding dirt bikes, fixing cars, and getting his hands dirty. He drove a low-rider pickup truck and went hunting as a teen.

Jonathan took a blue-collar path, working physical labor jobs. He was a volunteer firefighter and delivered propane to low-income areas, often interacting with African American or Hispanic families.

Jonathan had one of the biggest hearts of anyone I'd ever met. He knew that when these families saw a white guy pulling up, they saw someone they didn't think could relate to them. Jonathan wanted to be able to talk to them and connect with them while the tanks were being filled. He even grew dreadlocks to put them at ease.

He was the kind of person who made other people feel seen, connected, and special. He deserved everything—but he had struggled along the way.

I would have financial conversations with Jonathan from time to time. His wife is an angel walking on the earth, and she handled the money. Early in their marriage after they had their first son, one of the things I knew he needed was life insurance. Jonathan and his wife banked with a large bank in town and his employer offered a family benefit package. When we saw each other at Christmas time, we walked through his options, and I showed him how important it was to purchase one of the available life insurance policies.

As it turned out, it was more important than either of us realized.

I will never forget the day I got the call. I was sitting on the beach enjoying a relaxing Friday afternoon with my wife Leigh Ana trying to start an early weekend. I was on a call with a client, Betty, talking about her finances, when Mom's phone number popped up on my phone.

I kept speaking with Betty but another call came in, then another. A bit worried, I told Betty that I needed to call her back.

I called my mom back. Whit, my stepfather (also an angel walking on earth who always has a way of being very direct) answered.

He gave me news I never thought I would hear. In fact, I cannot really remember the exact words he said. The message was clear though: Jonathan had died, suddenly and tragically, in a head-on car wreck at just 41 years old in our hometown.

At Jonathan's funeral, there was a massive turnout—people from everywhere, both sides of town, all races, and all ages. People he inspired. People he *saw*. People could feel how special he was in every interaction. At the funeral, there was a black-and-white image on the screen of Jonathan wearing a bandana and sunglasses, his hair in free flow mode. The caption read, "Ask me about him."

(That message, "Ask me about him" found its way on t-shirts. They are still worn around our hometown as a testament to his one-of-a-kind life and his impact on those he loved.)

I looked around and I knew that Jonathan's legacy was going to live on, shared by all of these people whose lives he had touched.

Before the service, I visited with him one last time in an empty sanctuary. I remember standing in front of the casket, looking down at his face, in awe. Through my tears, I told him, "Jonathan, you truly lived a one-of-a-kind life."

I also made him a promise. "I will always work to be different—just like you."

I knew after witnessing his funeral that if I wanted to inspire, to lead, to impact people, to change things, to leave this world a better place than it was before me, then I had to be willing to show up differently. I had to break away from the traditional mold of thinking and do anything and everything I could to make sure my clients were able to do the same.

Jonathan built a one-of-a-kind life. He created a vision (more on that in Chapter 11) that included connecting with his customers, his neighbors, and his church. And the financial plan we created supported that vision. Jonathan's plan didn't just give him the life he dreamed of, though. It also left a *legacy*. The life insurance they had purchased is what allows his family to live *their* lives the way Jonathan wanted them to, to travel and to be free of worry. That policy still provides for his family, giving them opportunities and enriching their lives, even after his death—and that's exactly what Jonathan would have wanted.

Jonathan did more in his 41 years than most people do in a lifetime, and the impact he left lives on in our hearts and in our actions. I believe that we have two deaths: The first is the day we die. And the second is the last day our names are spoken on this earth. Jonathan has had his first death, but his name lives on. His legacy lives on. His one-of-a-kind life lives on. It inspires those who knew him. It inspires our family, his wife, and their kids. And it inspires me, shaping how I show up every single day.

YOUR ONE-OF-A-KIND LIFE

Jonathan and Connie's stories are marked by unexpected loss of life. I don't share these stories to scare you. But I do hope they light a fire under you.

The truth is, we're not promised tomorrow. But whether you have one more day of life or 60 more years, I know that you deserve to live *your life* with more of what you want. And I know that a One of a Kind Financial Plan™ will help you do that.

This belief is what I have poured into each of my clients (and into all of the pages that follow). It is how I've helped them reach the lives they want sooner, instead of waiting for a day that might not ever come.

There's Sarah and Patrick, who were high school sweethearts who worked for the Coast Guard. They wanted to share as much time together in this world as possible for as long as possible. We were able to grow their net worth to the point that they were able to retire to Florida, where they can soak up the sun and the love they share for the rest of their days.

Then there's Melanie, who had a truly one-of-a-kind dream. She wanted to spend her days researching the Salem Witch Trials. That was what she wanted most out of life— and we were able to plan her finances to set her up to make that dream possible.

Your one-of-a-kind life will not look like anyone else's. Maybe you have some things in common with one of these clients…or maybe your ideal life is completely different.

Maybe you want to spend your days on the beach, lounging by the ocean. Maybe you want to explore old castles. Maybe you want to write a book. Maybe you want to go back to school and pursue a second or third career you never thought was possible. Maybe you want to spend time with your kids—or your grandkids, providing childcare for them to carry your legacy forward.

Whatever it is, I know that a One of a Kind Financial Plan™ can help you get there sooner with more security, ensuring your money grows in the most strategic way possible to secure the life that you want to live.

As you read on and begin to understand what it takes to craft that One of a Kind Financial Plan™, I encourage you to think about what makes *you* one of a kind. Visualize the life that you want—not the life you think you "should" live. Because *that* (not the money itself) is the key to happiness.

CHAPTER 2

BUILD A PLAN TO SUIT YOUR LIFE!

I'm not in the business of giving people advice that I don't follow myself. The one-of-a-kind method isn't *just* something I offer or teach. It's the way I approach my life, because I'm determined to carry on my brother's legacy and to live in a truly unique way. And it isn't something just for me—it's an approach to life I've built into my entire family. Every Milligan lives a one-of-a-kind life.

Take my youngest daughter, for example. Before starting college, she took a gap year to travel the world. Cambodia, Thailand, South Africa, Guatemala. She did things most people never have the opportunity to do in their lives. She hiked an active volcano. She bungee jumped off the largest bungee bridge in the world. She lived in a tent for 60 days. She survived for nine months on only what she could carry in a backpack. She soaked up the world and drank every minute of that year.

Then there's my middle child who played four years of college soccer at a NCAA ranked school where she served as captain. On the profile of the team's roster page, each player listed a career objective. My daughter's goal was "to save the earth." And after graduating college, she took an internship at a nonprofit in Alabama so she could do just that. She moved states away, leaving the comforts of her home to chase down her dream. I remember the day she packed up everything she owned into her little Fiat 500x and headed toward her future.

Just ten minutes outside of Birmingham on her initial descent into town, she called me and asked, "Dad, am I crazy?"

I told her, "Probably. But are you scared?"

She was honest and said yes.

I said, "Good."

I wanted her to be a little uncomfortable but not afraid of pushing out of her comfort zone and living her one-of-a-kind life. And I'm proud to say my daughter is thriving. She works at a nonprofit, solving the needs of the poor, disadvantaged, and underprivileged. She finds ways to take perfectly good food that stores can't sell and gets it into the hands of people who need it most. From there, the food that can't be eaten by humans finds its way to farms for animals or into compost for fertilizing future food. She is helping the world—forgoing huge financial gains yet using the money she earns strategically to live a life that lights her up.

And then there's my son—living his one-of-a-kind life completely differently from his sisters. He's a husband. He's a father. And he's also going through medical school. Any one of those things is all consuming. But he's doing it all, and he would not change a thing.

My wife and I travel together—disconnecting from

work and conquering personal challenges of our choice, like hiking Machu Picchu and Rainbow Mountain (more on that later). We have island hopped in the Caribbean. We have taken trains and boats around Europe to see that there is beauty in old things. And National Parks get the best reaction out of my wife, like when she spotted a water buffalo in the wild for the first time. We set our sights on the next experience we want to create together and make it happen.

The point is that living a one-of-a-kind life isn't something we talk about—it's something we do. The Milligans do it.

But the bigger point is that while we're all living that one-of-a-kind life we want, we also know that none of it happens by accident.

To live your life fully, you need to plan fully.

> *To live your life fully, you need to plan fully.*

Without a One of a Kind Financial Plan™, we wouldn't be able to live these lives. My daughter wouldn't have been able to take a gap year and afford a trip around the world if I hadn't planned early, set aside a certain amount for her college, and been aware enough to help her figure out how to shift savings and finances around to make her trip a reality.

My other daughter wouldn't have had the savings to be able to uproot her life to Alabama for her dream nonprofit job. My son wouldn't have been able to go to medical school and still support a family. These things didn't happen by accident. And in my own journey, to get to where I am now—rising up from my small-town roots in a family struggling to make ends meet—took intention, planning, and commitment.

My One of a Kind Financial Plan™ has created these opportunities for each of us. It doesn't just impact me or how I'm going to live when I retire. It's how I show up now. It's how my kids are able to thrive in the world. It's the kind of life my grandkids are going to have. It's my legacy.

Your one-of-a-kind life isn't the same as mine. It might have similar elements, but it needs to be full of what makes YOU happy, fulfilled, and passionate. It's full of the pieces that are going to create your legacy—and that legacy begins with a One of a Kind Financial Plan™.

So, how do you know a One of a Kind Financial Plan™ is right for you?

You're in the right place if you:

- Have controlled your debt and are earning a stable income.
- Have been saving for retirement but you're not sure if you're doing it "right."
- You're just starting your retirement planning journey and have serious questions.

Those are the basics. But there are two other key components you need to get the most out of this book:

1. You need to be ready to embrace your dream life (even if you've never envisioned it before).
2. You need to be willing to hear that what you have *been doing* financially might not be the best way to get there.

BUILD A PLAN TO SUIT YOUR LIFE!

The bottom line? *The One of a Kind Financial Plan*™ is for people who want to live a one-of-a-kind life.

It isn't about saving X dollars per year, following hard and fast rules, or just blindly accruing money and hoping you have enough later down the line. It's about taking control of your future *now* by:

- Reducing your taxes over your life.
- Freeing up your money.
- Setting up your retirement income as soon as possible.
- Investing in things that actually align with your values and life.
- Setting up your long-term care plan so that you're not a burden to those you love the most.
- And establishing a legacy that is so well-organized that it becomes not just a set of legal documents but an I Love You letter to those that matter to you most.

If that sounds overwhelming, don't worry. I'm going to walk you through it step by step.

- 29 -

CHAPTER 3

WHAT'S HOLDING YOU BACK FROM YOUR ONE-OF-A-KIND LIFE?

Living a one-of-a-kind life sounds incredible, doesn't it? Maybe now you're starting to envision what it might look like for you. You're contemplating different pieces of it, like traveling, or spending time with family. Maybe there's something in the back of your mind just waiting to come forward, ready to be a part of your future.

But in my experience with clients, it's actually much harder to truly, clearly envision your one-of-a-kind life than you could ever imagine. It usually takes quite a bit of questioning and drawing out the vision before you can even allow yourself to think differently.

That's why with my clients, I start with the life piece, meaning creating the vision for their one-of-a-kind life. The numbers are easier—though that may be hard to believe. **The vision is the hard part!**

There are two sets of barriers most of my clients face when trying to create their one-of-a-kind lives. In this chapter we'll talk about barriers to envisioning your *one-of-a-kind life*. Then, in the next chapter, we'll tackle barriers to creating your *One of a Kind Financial Plan*™.

BARRIERS TO ENVISIONING YOUR ONE-OF-A-KIND LIFE

When it comes down to it, there are usually two barriers standing in the way of creating a one-of-a-kind life.

Barrier #1: Fear of the Unknown

What I'm asking you to do can feel like a challenge because it directly challenges the way you've been conditioned to think, probably since the time that you were a child. And at some level, I'm going to guess there's a lingering fear of dreaming bigger, a fear of thinking differently, a fear of breaking the mold.

We aren't trained to think differently. Instead, we're trained to work Monday through Friday, from nine to five, with four weeks of vacation a year (or less), for forty years or more.

We trade our time, working for someone else, and we believe that hard work will eventually lead us to where we need to be. But in the process, we often put our lives on hold. We might even sacrifice our time, our values, and our identities, trying to climb corporate ladders and earn more money, thinking that eventually that will give us what we want.

All of those hours spent working for other people, without thinking about where we're heading or what we want, are hours we're not spending creating or living a one-of-a-kind life. And the sad truth is that if you were to die, your employer would replace you in a week. Your time would be lost, and they would move right along.

> *You can choose to think differently—to ask yourself what it is that you really want.*

But it doesn't have to be that way. You can choose to think differently—to ask yourself what it is that you really want. Not what you think you're "supposed" to do. Not what everyone else around you is doing. Not just following the path you think you've been given. You can choose to live the life that you know gives you meaning—one without regrets and missed opportunities and endless sacrifice.

Barrier #2: Not Having a Clear Vision

The other big challenge we face in living a one-of-a-kind life is not taking the time to envision it. When we're stuck in our day-to-day obligations, we don't take the time to ask ourselves where we're really headed or whether it's somewhere we want to be.

Before we know it, we arrive at "Retirement," a destination we've been told to look forward to. We might imagine resting in a recliner, free from agendas and obligations. And that all might sound great until you realize that retirement is just an endless loop of consecutive Saturdays over and over and over again. And without knowing how you want to spend your days, without that clear vision, without a purpose, it's a lot harder to live a one-of-a-kind life.

You might realize this isn't what you want to be doing, scrambling to reconnect with the dreams you've sidelined, recognizing that you haven't set yourself up to be able to achieve them.

That's why you need a plan with vision, so you aren't in the endless Saturday loop without knowing where you're going next. Rest and relaxation might be part of the dream, but they're not everything. Humans need purpose.

To live a retirement with purpose, a one-of-a-kind life that fulfills you, you need something I like to call Retirement CHI™.

FINDING YOUR RETIREMENT CHI™

In Chinese philosophy, *chi* represents life force: a vital flow of energy. During retirement, finding your chi involves focusing on three pillars: Community, Health, and Impact. Visualizing these elements helps shape your one-of-a-kind life.

Community: Your one-of-a-kind life in retirement needs a community. It might mean friends, family, a church, a club. Even if you're introverted, you need some level of social interaction and a sense of belonging—a place where you can be yourself. Community is essential

What are the interests that you hope to pursue, rediscover, or maintain...are there communities, clubs, or groups built around these interests? Will you have family living nearby that you will spend time with? Will you meet up with a group of friends every month for breakfast or coffee? How will you go about creating a community for yourself?

These are important things to visualize clearly and questions to ask. Things might change between now and then, but when you're clear about the life you want to live and your Retirement CHI™, you can make sure those changes are still working toward the life you want. No matter how things change, community will still matter. You will still need people around you to connect with, to share your time with, and to build that all-important place where you belong.

Health: Your health is the cornerstone of the life you want to live, especially as you age. Think about how you want to maintain your health and then live that lifestyle you want for as long as possible.

What purpose does your health serve? What does it allow you to do? Do you envision yourself taking up biking or running marathons? Dancing? Riding horses? Spending time outdoors, hiking and communing in nature? What helps keep your physical and mental health in optimal condition? Is it playing with your grandkids? Gardening? What is that thing that makes you wake up energized?

Whatever your answers to these questions are, we know that our health is something we need to invest in now. If you want to be active when you're 85, you can't wait until you're 65 to start stretching and exercising. You need to focus on your health today, or one day your health will become your only focus.

It's no different from our main topic in this book—your finances. You need to be creating the investment in your health *now* so you can achieve and do what you want in the future.

Impact: The final piece is the most important—your impact. This is the purpose of the life you live in retirement.

When you're working, you can see the impact you make, whether positive or negative. It doesn't matter what job you do—you have an impact on others around you, and it's easy to recognize. In fact, it's what keeps you coming back to a job or ultimately looking for a new one. If you feel unfulfilled in your work, like you're not making some sort of impact, you'll likely seek a position where you can make a difference.

But we often overlook the fact that we still need to make an impact in retirement—and that impact is often harder to see.

The impact you have on the world will ultimately become your legacy. What impact is it that you want to have? How will you contribute to society? It can be on a micro or a macro level, but it's critical to find a purpose bigger than yourself and work to make a difference.

This could be as simple as volunteering to garden the neighborhood common spaces. Or it might be mentoring underprivileged kids. Maybe it's housing international students for exchange programs or watching your grandchildren so your kids avoid the cost of daycare. You become a part of the next generation, actively contributing to your legacy.

Only you can decide what impact you want to have. But I urge you to take the time to consider what it is now, to visualize what it's going to look like, and think about what you need to do to get there.

REFLECTION EXERCISE: YOUR RETIREMENT CHI™

It's time to start visualizing your Retirement CHI™ and where you want to be in the future.

If you could retire tomorrow, what would you want your life to look like? Write down three things you would want for each piece of Retirement CHI™:

Community:

Your Health:

Your Impact:

VISUALIZING YOUR ONE-OF-A-KIND LIFE

Mapping out your Retirement CHI™, and ultimately your one-of-a-kind life, both today and in retirement, isn't just a mental exercise for fun. It isn't just about dreaming. It's about lighting a fire under you to create the one-of-a-kind plan that's going to get you there. When you know the life that's waiting for you, you'll be in a hurry to build the plan to create it.

In Part 3 of this book, I will walk you through the steps you need to take to create your One of a Kind Financial Plan™. But before you can even get to that point, you have to be able to envision what your dream life looks like.

In addition to the three pillars in your Retirement CHI™, your one-of-a-kind life should be built around five core elements—the highest priorities or values that matter most to you above all else. These are the things that make your life truly one-of-a-kind.

It might be the thrill of travel, savoring great food, enjoying fine wine, or nurturing deep relationships with friends or a spouse. For others, it could be about growing a business to its fullest potential, participating in marathons, or championing a cause.

Whatever it is, it starts with your values and your priorities. The problem is that no one ever asks us to define those. Right now, I'm going to ask you.

REFLECTION QUESTIONS

Take a few minutes to answer these questions. Write them down and get clear. Your answers will become the basis of your vision for your one-of-a-kind life:

1. *Why is money important to you?*

2. *What excites you every day?*

3. *What gets you out of bed in the morning?*

4. *What would you do if you knew you never had to worry about money?*

5. *What is something you're never late for because you genuinely want to be there?*
6. *What brings a smile to your face whenever you think about it?*
7. *What feels effortless and doesn't seem like work?*
8. *What do you hope your children, grandchildren, or friends will remember about you after you're gone?*
9. *Where would you escape to if you could go anywhere?*
10. *Where do you feel most at peace?*
11. *What could you happily do every day?*

Answering these questions will help define your one-of-a-kind life. And if you can't align your financial goals with this vision, then what are you saving money for? Are you saving just to accumulate wealth? If your answer is yes, then we have work to do. Accumulating wealth is entirely different from creating your one-of-a-kind life.

Remember, at the end of the day, we're all bankrupt. Meaning, you'll leave this world with nothing. Sure, your money might go to your family—and there's nothing wrong with that intention. But are you here to fulfill someone else's wish list? Or are you here to say that you matter enough to live the life you want? You are the one who has the choice. You get to decide.

My greatest hope is that you decide that you are worthy of a one-of-a-kind life.

SELF CHECK-IN: HOW CLEAR IS YOUR VISION?

Before we go further, let's take a minute to check in on your vision for your one-of-a-kind life. For each of the following statements, rate yourself on a scale from 1–5, where 1 means "not accurate at all" and 5 means "very accurate." Then, add up your score and use the score interpretation section that follows to evaluate how clearly you have defined your one-of-a-kind life.

I have a clear understanding of my personal priorities and what is most important to me.	
I can describe what my dream retirement looks like in detail.	
I can describe what my dream life before retirement looks like in detail.	
I regularly take time to reflect on my priorities and adjust them as necessary.	
I know what activities or experiences bring me the most joy and fulfillment.	
I have specific goals for myself that I want to achieve (for example, writing a book, or visiting every continent).	
I know what kind of legacy I want to leave behind.	
I feel that my current lifestyle is moving me in the direction of my long-term vision for life.	
I have spoken in detail with a trusted person in my life about what I want in the immediate and long-term future.	
I make choices in my life based on the vision I want for myself.	
I have thought about how to achieve my vision and started working toward it.	
I am comfortable living life on my own terms instead of trying to fit into a mold.	

I am able to easily answer questions about what I want to do with my life or where I envision myself in the future.	
I have defined my Retirement CHI™ (what my community, health, and impact look like in retirement).	
I know why money is important to me and how I want to use it in my life.	

Score Interpretation

1–25: Your life vision might feel vague or undefined. You might not have considered what your one-of-a-kind life would look like nor even given yourself permission to think bigger. If you have a financial plan in place, it likely isn't created with your future in mind and you might be missing opportunities to control your financial future. This book can help you build the knowledge you need, the vision you want, and the plan to get there. Take time to reflect on what matters most to you—and consider seeking a financial professional who can help you understand how your financial plan can help you work toward your one-of-a-kind life.

26–50: You have a general sense of what you want but may need to refine it further. You likely haven't created a plan to get there. If you have a financial plan in place, it's likely a traditional model, not one established with your one-of-a-kind life in place. You need some clarity on your vision of how to get there. This book will help you firm up the vision, identify the gaps in your current financial plan, and develop a simple roadmap to course correct.

51–75: You have strong clarity around your one-of-a-kind life vision. Congratulations, you're further along than most people! But now the question is, do you have a One of a Kind Financial Plan™ to support it? The next chapter will help you answer this question, and the rest of this book can give you the tools you need to support the life that you have envisioned.

CHAPTER 4

THE BARRIERS TO CREATING YOUR ONE OF A KIND FINANCIAL PLAN™

Now that you know the barriers to envisioning your one-of-a-kind life, it's time to talk about the barriers that stand in the way of creating your One of a Kind Financial Plan™.

Barrier #1: Disorganization

When I ask new clients about their finances, I often hear the same story: "Well, I think I have something in a 401(k)… there's an IRA somewhere. I know I have an account with Fidelity—I just haven't logged in for a while because I forgot my password." Sound familiar?

It used to be a shoebox full of receipts and papers, everything shoved into a box to be dumped out in front of a financial professional. It's still a shoebox, but it's online.

It's easy to understand how this happens. Life gets busy. Accounts from old jobs or investments are forgotten. We're consumed with what's in front of us—kids, sports, caregiving, and our careers. And the things that don't seem immediately pressing, like retirement accounts, slip through the cracks.

We all have a junk drawer in our kitchen—the place where we shove random things we know we need but not right now. We can't be organized in all areas of our lives at all times. But keeping your financial plan in a junk drawer doesn't work.

If this is ringing bells for you, and if this has held you back from getting a financial plan in place in the past, I want you to know that this barrier is easy to overcome. Disorganization isn't a personal failing; it's human. You don't need to be embarrassed. You don't have to know where everything is. A trusted financial planner can help you make sense of your finances, build organization into your plan, and stick to it. Getting organized can be simple if you're doing it with somebody who has the experience to see where you are and to get you to where you want to be.

SELF CHECK-IN: FINANCIAL ORGANIZATION

Take a few minutes to evaluate how organized your finances are currently. Answer whether the following questions are true or false for you:

I regularly check in on the total value of my financial assets and can always give an accurate ballpark of my net worth.	
I know where all of my accounts are located.	
I know roughly how much money is in each of my accounts.	

I can easily log into all of my financial accounts (bank, retirement, investments) and regularly do so.	
I track my spending and understand my monthly expenses.	
I know what's included in my investment portfolio.	
I have a clear savings plan for my future goals.	
I have an up-to-date will.	
I have minimized or eliminated debt and have a plan to manage any remaining balances.	
I know what my company's match is and how much is being put into my accounts on a regular basis.	
I feel confident discussing my financial situation with a financial professional.	
I have a plan for my long-term care in place.	
I know the cost of my current investment plan.	
I have an emergency fund and know how I would handle it if a big expense occurred right now.	
I have a written record of my finances that is easy to understand.	
I know WHY I am growing my wealth and how it relates to my one-of-a-kind life.	

If you've answered "false" to *any* of these, you probably need to create some changes. If you answered mostly true, you're on the right track, but there might still be some other barriers at play holding you back from your strongest financial plan.

Barrier #2: The "It's too Much Work" Myth

Another common barrier to creating a financial plan is the myth that it's too much work or will take too long. So under that pretense, we end up putting it off because we get overwhelmed.

But creating a smart financial plan doesn't have to be as time-consuming as you might think. Let me share the story of Russell and Peggy, a couple I recently worked with. Peggy, a recovering veterinarian, was burnt out after years of grueling work, and Russell was a federal employee. When they came to me, they felt overwhelmed and unsure where to start, believing that to gather everything to do with their finances would take forever.

What if I told you we built their entire plan in just three hours spread across one year? That's all it took—three 45-minute meetings and 15 minutes of homework each time we met. Now, they've saved $7,000 annually in taxes, lowered investment fees, and created a will and trust.

The point is, it doesn't take forever. It just takes intention. If you're up against the myth that "it takes too much time," you have three choices:

Option #1: You can keep letting financial planning slip to the back burner, telling yourself it can wait, and never reach your one-of-a-kind life.

Option #2: You can do the work to get things organized and in place by yourself, investing many hours of effort that will be well worth it in the long run.

Option #3: Work with a financial planner who can help you and invest just a few hours like Russell and Peggy did.

You can't keep shoving everything into the proverbial financial junk drawer, literally or figuratively. It's easy to think financial planning can wait. But the truth is, *it can't wait.* You need to start taking steps to plan now. The more proactive you are, the less time it will take to stay organized in the long run.

Barrier #3: Shame About Revealing Failures

Most people know that they need support to create a savvy financial plan. But some hold back from working with a financial professional. Why? Because they are holding onto shame about their past financial mistakes.

This includes things like a bad investment, overwhelming debt, a decision that cost you financially, a loan you regret, or a debt that feels insurmountable. But I'm here to tell you, none of these circumstances should hold you back.

Many of us grew up with taboos or shame around money—whether it was not having enough, or the belief that money shouldn't be discussed. We weren't always given the best blueprint for a healthy relationship with money. And when we're carrying that money belief baggage and then we experience mistakes or unfortunate circumstances, we might want to ignore it and sweep it under the rug so no one sees it.

Here's the truth—you will get nowhere pretending everything's fine. You don't have to be ashamed of the mistakes you've made in the past. In fact, honesty is your superpower. There are three people in this world you should always tell the truth to—your priest, your doctor, and your financial planner (and if you're married, your spouse).

> *There are three people in this world you should always tell the truth to—your priest, your doctor, and your financial planner.*

Lay it all out on the table. A good financial partner doesn't judge; they guide. They're your ally. They're the person that's going to have your back and help you work forward from the mistakes instead of letting them continue to negatively impact you.

I worked with a couple, Linda and Scott, who came in with a list of creditors longer than a buffet table. They wanted to retire and move to western Virginia, and they didn't know how to make this dream a reality. But they were open, honest, and willing to share the truth of their debt. We worked together over eight years to minimize their debt and help them live their dream.

If you're on the fence about working with a financial professional because you're afraid to share your failures, think about this. When you ignore a problem, does it get bigger or does it get smaller? Think about it. If you don't address your tax bill, it will only increase. The same goes for any financial problems—ignoring them won't make them disappear—they tend to only grow.

You don't have to tackle your financial planning alone. You need someone in your corner who will be as honest with you as you should be with them. You might need to make adjustments. There might be some goals that are out of reach. But there is a path to a one-or-a-kind life for you. Don't be ashamed or think it's too late. There's always a path forward.

DEFINE THE LIFE, DEFINE THE PLAN

What I want you to know is this: all the fears you're holding onto—the ones that are keeping you from starting to build your one-of-a-kind life—and all the barriers standing in the way of you living the life you really want to live…they're solvable. And the solution *is* the One of a Kind Financial Plan™.

> When you have the plan in place, it eliminates the fear, the uncertainty, the stress, and the what-ifs.

When you have the plan in place, it eliminates the fear, the uncertainty, the stress, and the what-ifs. It gives you the power to take control of what you *can* control and build in security for what you can't control, so that you can live your life without fear or worry, knowing that you have prepared for your future and are ready to live life on your terms. And defining your one-of-a-kind life is what gives you the focus you need to create the plan that makes sense for you.

So often, people approach financial professionals as if they're a retail store, wanting to peruse the shelves and shop for products, without ever understanding why or if they need them.

My big question for you to reflect on is: If you don't know what your one-of-a-kind life looks like or why the money you have saved and invested is important to you, what's the point of the plan? What's the point of the work you're putting in? What's the point of any of it?

You can't just wing your financial future and hope you stumble into the life you want. Every asset, every decision, every investment, every account—they're part of your one-of-a-kind life. The choices you make right now dictate your future.

I hope that you decide that you are worth the investment, that your one-of-a-kind life is worth overcoming these barriers and getting your financial plan started. And I hope that you always decide to be true to your one-of-a-kind self.

CHAPTER 5

NAVIGATING THE FINANCIAL MINEFIELD: HOW DO YOU KNOW WHO TO TRUST?

In Chapters 3 and 4, I walked you through the internal barriers—the fears, the embarrassment, and the uncertainty—that hold people back from working toward a one-of-a-kind life, including taking the steps to create a One of a Kind Financial Plan™. But once you've overcome those pieces, you're going to face perhaps your biggest challenge yet: knowing who to trust and who to listen to.

Maybe you're reading this book right now, thinking to yourself, "How do I even know Mike is giving me good advice?"

It's a legitimate question. After all, if you've tried to get financial answers before, you've probably landed right in the middle of a minefield of financial uncertainty.

Picture this: You're standing at a crossroads, holding a map that's supposed to lead you to financial freedom. The trouble is, the map is covered in arrows going in all directions, and there are ten different people shouting at you, each insisting their path is the only way to go. Some promise security, others boast about huge returns, and then there's the guy holding a giant sign that says, "BUY GOLD!" The noise is overwhelming, and all you want is someone to point you in the right direction.

Maybe you've consulted a professional financial advisor. Maybe you've been scrolling TikTok, listening to self-proclaimed finance "gurus." Either way, you've probably heard conflicting opinions. Some advisors push life insurance. Others focus on mutual funds. Some gurus might claim cryptocurrency is your one golden ticket. Even within the same financial universe, no two advisors will necessarily give you the same advice.

The advice is confusing. It's intimidating. And everyone seems to have an agenda. No wonder so many people end up stuck in "analysis paralysis," too overwhelmed by all the information online to make the next move.

But navigating this minefield requires more than just direction—you need clarity. Who can you trust? And how do you separate genuine guidance from polished sales pitches designed to push a product rather than serve your best interests?

THE #1 DECEPTION IN THE FINANCIAL INDUSTRY

If you've dabbled at all in working with a financial professional, you've probably heard the term "fiduciary." The technical definition of fiduciary is that an advisor is legally bound to prioritize your best interests. It sounds amazing, right? Who wouldn't want someone like that handling their money?

So it's no wonder that the first question people ask when they call my office or reach out to me is often, "Are you a fiduciary?"

The trouble is that what fiduciary is *supposed* to mean and what it actually means is far from the same. There are a lot of people out there calling themselves fiduciaries who are anything but. They'll tell you what they think your "best" solution is, but it's always going to be limited to the *products they're licensed to sell.*

> *There are a lot of people out there calling themselves fiduciaries who are anything but.*

You can go to a "fiduciary" life insurance agent. They're going to tell you that an indexed universal life insurance policy (IUL), the only product they're licensed to sell, is the answer to your problems.

Indexed Universal Life (IUL): A life insurance policy with a cash value that grows based on stock market performance.

You can go to a "fiduciary" broker who's licensed to sell mutual funds and variable annuities. They're going to tell you that mutual funds or annuities are the answers to your problems.

Mutual Funds: A pool of money collected from multiple investors to invest in securities like stocks, bonds, or other assets. Managed by a professional, mutual funds provide diversification, making them a popular choice for many investors. Keep in mind, fees and market performance can affect returns.

Annuity: A financial contract offered by life insurance companies that offers benefits to meet your financial needs.

You can go to a bank and meet with a "fiduciary" employee there. They're going to tell you that bank CDs or any of the other products they sell are the answer to your problems.

Certificates of Deposit (CDs): A savings account with a fixed interest rate and maturity date. You agree to leave your money in the account for a set term, and in return, the bank pays you higher interest than a regular savings account. However, withdrawing early may result in penalties.

These people probably aren't villains. They might be well-intentioned. Most of them aren't out to intentionally take advantage of you or lead you astray. But the problem is that these advisors are trained to make a profit for the company they work for, and therefore to see their products as the answer: for you and for everyone else who walks through their door.

That's why I believe the biggest lie the financial industry has sold is the concept of "fiduciary." How can those people claim to have your best interests in mind? If they can't offer *all* the solutions, how can they call themselves a fiduciary?

If financial advisors are strictly limited to the tools they are licensed to sell, their version of "best interest" boils down to what works best within their business model—not necessarily what's best for you.

So, am I a fiduciary? Technically, yes. Are there solutions I do not get paid to offer? Yes. But I will still make sure you are aware of them. *This transparency* is what we're missing in the industry.

WHOSE BURGER IS BETTER?

Think about it like this. A burger is, at its core, a simple concept: a bun, a patty, some toppings, and sauces. It's not complicated. But every burger chain has its own spin on it.

Take McDonald's. Their Big Mac is the same no matter where you go. California, New York, Florida, overseas—it's always two all-beef patties, special sauce, lettuce, cheese, pickles, onions, on a sesame seed bun. And that's great—you know exactly what you're getting.

Now, compare that with Burger King's Whopper. The ingredients are similar, but their message? "Have it your way." Customize it however you like. Their entire marketing strategy is to be what McDonald's is not.

And then there's Five Guys. Still a burger, but now you've got even more choices—lettuce, grilled onions, jalapeños, and even premium toppings like avocado or bacon.

Burger joints generally compete by highlighting what makes their burger great. They don't waste time bad-mouthing the competition—they just explain why you should choose them. They compete in the space because they know that a good American loves a burger.

The financial space is similar to the burger space but with one major difference. Everyone's doing burgers. They follow the same process for everybody who walks in the door. Annuities. IULs. Mutual funds. However, they make their burger (i.e., their income), that's what you get—same as everyone else in front of you in line, same as everyone else behind you. But instead of just telling you why their burger is great, they try to convince you that every other competitor's ingredients are toxic. Some brokers will tell you that life insurance is a "terrible investment." Some life insurance agents will assure you that annuities are "awful." They'll act like everyone else is out to get you and their product is the golden ticket for your financial future.

The professionals who work with a standardized approach, like McDonald's or Burger King, in the financial space are frontline soldiers for a corporate brand. They're there to sell burgers, collect a paycheck, and get promoted. And they do that by telling you that their burger is the *only* *one* worth buying.

They're going to use math and charts and a script they've been given to show you how your money can grow best using their method and their method only. And it's going to sound convincing. It's going to sound like you're getting served the best burger in the world. But at the end of the day, it's just a Big Mac. It's a one-size-fits-all approach.

So...what's the answer? It's not that burgers are bad and you should avoid them all. But in the financial world, it does mean that you can't always trust the advice you're hearing—the person giving it to you is trained (and paid) to tell you that their one-size-fits-all solution is the only solution.

WHO'S WHO OF FINANCIAL PROFESSIONALS

So, how *do* you know who to trust? It starts with understanding who you're talking to.

Financial professionals aren't all the same. They don't offer the same products, and they don't work the same way. Here are some of the types you might encounter:

- **Investment Advisory Representatives/Financial Advisors:** They sell investments and charge annual fees for asset management. They are only licensed to sell securities and are regulated by the SEC (the Securities and Exchange Commission: the United States government agency in charge of monitoring the financial markets).
- **Brokers:** They earn commissions from the products they sell, such as mutual funds or variable annuities. They are only licensed to sell a limited number of products and are regulated by FINRA (the Financial Industry Regulatory Authority: a nonprofit organization designed specifically to monitor brokers).
- **Insurance Agents:** They earn commissions from the sale of life insurance and fixed insurance products. They are only licensed to sell non-stock market financial instruments. They are regulated by state insurance regulators.

- **Financial Entertainers**: Think Dave Ramsey, Suze Orman, etc. They aren't licensed to do anything. They do provide an entrance into financial education, and they have some good insight. But they are NOT licensed to give you specific advice. That's why their tips often sound generic and overly simplified. At best, they can give you introductory knowledge. They can't sell you a product. And they definitely can't give you unique, specific advice that works for you.

Then, there's another group—**Certified Financial Planners (CFP®)**. With just over 100,000 globally, certified financial planning professionals are a rare breed. They are ethically bound to be *true* fiduciaries. They're trained to provide customized, independent advice and can offer a broad range of financial solutions. A good CFP® acts like a gourmet burger joint. They listen, adapt, and craft a personalized "menu" that fits your unique taste.

It's important to note that not all CFP® professionals are created equal. Some work for big firms that prioritize corporate profits over client needs. Independent CFP® professionals aren't tied down by shareholder demands or boardroom agendas.

(I'm proud to be a CFP®, and I take the goal of being a true fiduciary seriously. I've taken my 25 years of experience in the industry to form a unique approach, and I believe that it can work for you. But if, as you work through this book, you don't decide to come work with me, at the very least, I urge you to find an independent CFP®: someone who is able to offer *a range* of solutions instead of just one product. You can find out more about CFP® professionals in the resources section of this book.)

HOW FINANCIAL PROFESSIONALS GET PAID

Now, we add another layer of complexity: how financial professionals make money. This is one of the most important things to understand because a person's paycheck can influence the advice they give.

Advisors typically fall into three categories when it comes to payment structures:

1. **Assets Under Management (AUM):**
   These advisors charge a percentage fee based on the total amount of investments they manage for you. For example, with $1 million under management and a 1% fee, they are paid $10,000 annually.

2. **Assets Under Contract (AUC):**
   This model involves commissions. If an advisor sells you a life insurance policy or annuity, they may get a one-time or ongoing commission tied to that product.

3. **Assets Under Influence:**
   This is where advisors influence your strategy without directly managing your investments. You're paying for their expertise, not specific actions they take with your money. This could be an annual fee or done pro bono.

Now...which one is better? The answer is that there is no one "best" way. Each has its pros and cons. But the bottom line? You should know how your advisor is getting paid. Ask any financial professional you talk to, "How do you get paid?" A trustworthy advisor should have no problem explaining it.

MAKING THE COMPLEX SIMPLE

We've all experienced money worries. "Am I doing this right? Can I trust what my advisor is telling me? What if I make the wrong move?" You're not alone. Financial minefields have been set up to make you feel like you need to rely on someone else because it's *too big* for you to figure out.

A major problem in the financial industry is that professionals are often selling you on concepts without considering the big picture concerning you and your one-of-a-kind life. Take life insurance, for example. Some life insurance agents can come with slick presentations. They'll show you charts and input some numbers to show you that a universal life insurance policy is *the answer* (the same presentation and the same script they're telling everyone else). And sure, those benefits can exist...but life insurance might not be right for everyone. Is it versatile? *Yes.* Is it something I recommend for many of my clients? *Absolutely.* Is it something everyone should own? *Absolutely not.* The same concept applies to all other financial products.

The truth is that no one asset is the golden ticket. Everything from CDs to cryptocurrency has beneficial attributes for the right investor, and at the same time, no product is right for everybody.

But you need to know what you're investing in, and why. And a good, trustworthy financial professional is going to help you cut through the noise and get there. I always say that if we can't make the complex simple, we don't deserve to be in this industry.

Creating your financial plan doesn't have to be complex, confusing, or even time-consuming. That's why I created the one-of-a-kind method. I've helped clients create their One of a Kind Financial Plan™ in just a matter of hours.

Now, maybe you're on board here. Maybe you haven't worked with a financial professional and you're ready to take this step.

Or maybe you already work with someone and you're thinking, "My financial advisor is great." And heck, maybe they are. But take a minute to ask yourself these reflection questions:

1. *Is my financial advisor asking me to describe the life I want now and in the future?*
2. *Is my financial advisor looking at the big picture of my finances with my one-of-a-kind life in mind?*
3. *Is my financial advisor making sure that I know exactly where my money is going—and why?*
4. *Is my financial advisor helping me mitigate taxes and free up money to grow for my future?*
5. *Is my financial advisor creating a plan that secures my taxes, investments, retirement income, long-term care planning, and the legacy I want to leave behind?*
6. *Is my financial advisor making sure that my money is being used for my priorities?*

If not, maybe you need someone else in your court.

CHAPTER 6

THE AMERICAN ~~DREAM~~ NIGHTMARE

In Chapter 5, I explained the different types of financial advisors and why the industry makes it so hard to find individualized, sound advice. But now, let's talk about how that minefield of advice actually holds you back from the life you want.

For decades, we've been chasing the American Dream: a home, financial security, and the freedom to enjoy the life you've worked hard for. But so many of us end up living the American Nightmare instead—uncertainty, frustration, and confusion about our finances and our future.

Why? Because while we've been sold the idea, we haven't been shown how to put all the pieces together. What should be the roadmap to our dream often becomes a chaotic process of trial and error that I call the Piecemeal Effect.

The Piecemeal Effect is the #1 reason why people don't end up where they want or need to be in retirement. It's why they never create a solid, strategic financial plan. It's why they work longer than they want to. And it's why they don't end up living the one-of-a-kind life they want.

THE PIECEMEAL EFFECT

Imagine this: You've just found the perfect plot of land to build your dream home. You're full of ideas about what this house should look like—the cozy kitchen, the spacious living room, the backyard where the kids can play or where you can host summer barbeques.

Now technically, you could go to The Home Depot to get everything you need. They sell the cinder blocks for the foundation, the lumber for the frame, the piping for the plumbing, and the shingles for the roof. Everything is available to you. But I'm guessing you wouldn't walk into Home Depot with a shopping cart and try to build your dream home by yourself.

Instead, you'd hire an architect to design the plan with you. They'd ask you about your family, your lifestyle, your day-to-day activities—and they'd work with you to create a home that fits that lifestyle. Essentially, you'd create a plan for your one-of-a-kind home together. Then you'd work with a builder who selects subcontractors to bring that blueprint to life.

Sure, those subcontractors will shop at Home Depot, but they're following a plan—and you end up with the home you want without rolling up your sleeves and trying to do the work yourself. If you had to do that, your dream home would become a construction site for disaster.

But that's exactly what happens in financial planning. You may already have all the right "parts." You might have a retirement account here, a life insurance policy there, even some mutual funds or Social Security strategies. You've talked to brokers, insurance agents, and maybe even tax preparers. Each has sold you a piece of the puzzle.

But without a plan, those pieces don't come together. You're left holding a pile of random materials, wondering how to turn them into the life you've dreamed of living.

And here's the kicker—you sought out professional help. Yet even the "experts" sent you shopping at the financial equivalent of The Home Depot.

This piecemeal financial approach does nothing but set you up for frustration. Insurance agents push their policies. Brokers sell stocks and funds. Tax preparers record last year's numbers but don't look ahead. You're getting fragments, and no one's stepping back to ask, "How does it all work together for you?"

The result? The American Dream becomes inaccessible. It's fragmented and disjointed. Instead of feeling empowered and confident to create the life you want, you're left trying to figure out how much money you need, how the individual pieces work together, and how to make sense of all of the pieces.

When I first started working in the industry, clients would walk in with a shoebox full of papers— crammed with mortgage statements, bank forms, retirement summaries, and random bits of information, asking me to create the dreamy retirement they wanted out of these scraps of paper.

Nowadays, we don't have the physical shoebox, but we haven't gotten any more organized. We essentially have digital shoeboxes that are still fragmented and disjointed. Nobody's taught you how to manage your lifetime tax bills, how to determine the income you need to live in retirement, how to evaluate your own risk, how to play the stock market, how to use life insurance policies strategically, how annuities work, how to build a legacy plan, or how all of it goes together.

At the end of the day, you've been given piecemeal advice to fill your box—and no way to make sense of it.

THE GET RICH SLOW ROAD

If you've fallen into the trap of the Piecemeal Effect, it's not your fault. You've done what you thought you were supposed to do. You trusted the system. You just didn't know you were being set up for the "Get-Rich-Slow" method by putting away money little by little, year after year.

So, you focused on other things. You went to school, pursued your career, paid your bills, maybe had a family, and focused on what was in front of you. And during all of that time, the key years for accumulating wealth, you didn't have time to become an expert in money.

Maybe you set aside money out of every paycheck. Maybe you saved as much as you could. Maybe you're invested through retirement accounts without really knowing what you're invested in or the tax implications of those investments.

And the truth is that if you make enough money, the Get-Rich-Slow road can get you *somewhere*. I see clients all the time who have managed to set aside $500,000, a million, or even more.

But they don't know what to do with it. They don't know if they have enough to support their retirement. They don't know how to make sure they're not going to run out of money. They don't know the best order to withdraw from their accounts or when to take out Social Security or how to mitigate their taxes. And they don't know how to take what they've worked hard for and build a life where they can actually live how they want to.

But that's where the One of a Kind Financial Plan™ is different. That's where working with *me* is different.

While you've been working in your zone of genius, working on your career, becoming an expert in what you do, I've been becoming an expert in what I do. I know how to give you enough financial education so that you know where your money is going and why. I know how to help you put everything together. **I know how to take the shoebox and turn it into a dream life.**

With the One of a Kind Financial Plan™, I'm not sending you to The Home Depot. I'm becoming your partner in building the dream, and I take that very seriously. I know that if I'm going to support my clients in their one-of-a-kind life, I need to really know them—their dreams, their struggles, and their fears. And I need to know every aspect of their finances through and through.

I worked with a couple, Maria and Jonah, who had followed the Get-Rich-Slow road. Jonah had worked steadily for 40 years, accumulating $700,000 in savings. Maria worked part-time and was looking forward to slowing down as well.

They wanted to sell their house, hit the road in an RV, and travel the United States. The steps to get there, however, weren't so clear. They didn't know how selling their house would impact their taxes, how much money they needed to support the RV lifestyle, or how to manage their accounts to create stable income.

Working together, we built a plan—one that accounted for their taxes, Social Security, investments, long-term healthcare, and estate planning. We created a safety net for emergencies. And we turned the money they'd saved into the life they wanted.

Maria and Jonah sold their home, purchased an RV, and spent the next two years living their dream. When their truck broke down in Tennessee, they didn't have to panic. They called me and asked, "Do we have room in the plan to buy a new truck?" Because we'd planned for emergencies, the answer was simple—yes. They replaced the truck and got back to their adventure with no sleepless nights.

Today, they're taking a break from the road to focus on their health. But the best part is, they're not stressing over finances. With a plan in place, they can continue living life on their terms.

FROM PIECEMEAL TO PEACE OF MIND

The Piecemeal Effect is the norm—but it doesn't have to be. You don't have to settle for the financial equivalent of a junk drawer. You deserve a beautiful, thoughtful plan that fits your life and your unique goals.

There's a better way to tackle your finances. There's a better way to plan for your future. There's a better way to put your hard work to good use.

The One of a Kind Financial Plan™ is comprehensive. It's proactive. It's designed to relieve the stress and the wondering and the worry and the sheer exhaustion that can come from dealing with finances by creating something different—something empowering, optimizing, and energizing.

When you create a One of a Kind Financial Plan™, you gain so much peace of mind. You know where you're going. You know how much money you'll need to get there. And to get there, you know the best choices you need to make, today, tomorrow, this year, and every year moving forward.

CHAPTER 7

THINKING DIFFERENTLY
ABOUT YOUR FINANCES

Everyone today knows the name Jeff Bezos and the brand Amazon. It's now the "Everything Store" where you can essentially buy whatever you want and have it at your home in a day or two. But that wasn't always the plan for Amazon.

When Bezos founded Amazon, he had a goal—to be the number one bookseller. He believed in the future of the Internet, and he thought that there was space to outsell big bookstores like Borders and Barnes & Noble. That's what he set out to do, working out of his garage with a small team. Before long, it took off.

He could have stopped there. The plan was good. It was doing what it was supposed to do. That could have been the end of the story—Amazon as a successful online bookstore. But Bezos let himself think bigger and see new possibilities.

He thought, "Okay, I have a great thing going here. What else can I do with this?" He started selling other things, eventually bringing in other sellers, a subscription service, streaming, and more. Now, Amazon is an iconic name— one of the top three companies in America.

His dream evolved into something that at one time never would have been imaginable. He gave himself the space to become iconic.

What is it that paved the way for this to happen? It was the ability to think differently, to think bigger, to think beyond what everyone else was doing. The same principle applies to financial planning.

A traditional financial plan is focused on hitting a "goal" of a specific number or retirement at a certain age. And that's essentially the end of the story. You put the plan into place, you save a set percentage a year, you set up the numbers to hit the goal—the end. It's the same one-size-fits-all approach that we've all been taught to follow.

But the One of a Kind Financial Plan™? That's the Amazon that Bezos dared to imagine. It isn't just checking off boxes to get to a number. It doesn't stop at "good enough." It evolves, bringing freedom and possibility to your life in ways you might not have initially imagined.

Here's the thing though—to get there, you have to be able to think differently. You have to be able to break away from the mold.

TOSSING OUT THE "GOAL"

I'm going to say something that you've probably never heard from a financial professional before. I'm *not* going to try to help you grow the biggest nest egg possible.

This is where the One of a Kind Financial Plan™ starts to diverge from what you've done before. I'm not just here to help you grow your money. In fact, if you follow the One of a Kind Financial Plan™, what you have left at the end of your life could be less than if you had gone the traditional route, depending on what your one-of-a-kind life looks like.

Traditional plans focus on how much your net worth can grow. You'll hear advisors tell you things like have a safe withdrawal rate of 4%, keep your money invested, and you'll end up with X amount of money. And guess what? In the end, your advisor has gotten the maximum. The bigger your nest egg, the bigger the fee the advisor has collected over your life.

But my goal isn't to have you only save and grow the maximum amount of money. The One of a Kind Financial Plan™ doesn't do that. It's not about a goal or a number. **It's not about how much you saved. It's about how much you lived.**

Have you used your money to live and do the things that are important to you? Have you used your wealth to travel and see the Great Wall of China or the Great Barrier Reef? Have you used it to invest time in your kids and grandkids? To support causes you believe in? To make your mark on the world so that your name lives forever?

That's why I believe the traditional financial approach leads people astray. It's also why I never ask a single client, "What's your goal?" Instead, I ask, "What's unique about you? Why is money important to you? What would you do if money wasn't a factor?"

We have to break away from the idea that there's this target to hit and that our job in life is to work until we reach it.

The one-size-fits-all approach just doesn't work. It leaves people focusing on the wrong things, and more importantly, it doesn't give them the security and confidence that they are going to be able to live the life they want without worries or fears.

Take the "4% safe withdrawal rule" for example. The idea *there* is that if you just withdraw 4% of your savings every year in retirement, you'll have enough to live off of it for 30 years or the rest of your life. But that magic number isn't as magic as it's made out to be. It's not based on your overall savings amount. It doesn't account for inflation. Even the creator of the 4% rule said that it wouldn't apply to everyone. It gets tossed around as if it's the golden rule of retirement—but it's simply not. What if 4% isn't enough to support your lifestyle? What if an emergency happens? What if you live more than 30 years?

Retirement "rules" don't account for any part of your actual individual life. And they do nothing to provide security or ease the fear that you might run out of money.

It's the same with all the other number goals or rules— get a nest egg of $1 million, put away 10% of your income every year, try to save up 12 times your pre-retirement salary, invest 100 minus your age in stocks. It's understandable that people would want a goal to aim for. But when the goal isn't based on you, when it's not carved out as part of an individualized financial plan, how can you ever rest easily or be assured that it's enough? That you'll be able to live the life you want? That you're covered even if you live longer than you expected, or if you travel, or even if you encounter medical concerns?

Some of those rules worked in the past, but they're based on outdated research and input from Wall Street gurus.

When traditional advisors try to offer one-size-fits-all approaches or number goals, they're essentially giving you 1970s solutions to 2025 problems. What we've seen time and time again is that the numbers don't always add up. Wall Street professionals were wrong yesterday, they're wrong today, and they'll be wrong tomorrow. They're focused on numbers instead of what people need as individuals.

Don't get me wrong, in a One of a Kind Financial Plan™, we're going to talk numbers. And of course I'm going to help you grow your wealth—but not so that it sits untouched in accounts while your life passes you by. Saving and investing and growing your money are all part of the One of a Kind Financial Plan™. But the difference is that you're saving and investing and growing your money with purpose—and you're spending it with purpose (and with the peace of mind that you have the funds available in place to do so).

In the One of a Kind Financial Plan™, numbers, money, and even the plan itself are just tools. They're not there to deprive you of life or keep you focused on a "goal." They're there to give you security, peace of mind, and the freedom to make your dream life a reality (even if those dreams change over time).

TURNING THE PLAN LOOSE

I attract people who don't fit the mold. They want unique things out of life. They fall outside of the box. And because of this, they don't fit the traditional financial advising model of work hard, save diligently, end up with as much money as possible, and leave a substantial inheritance for your heirs.

My client Leon is a great example. He is single, without kids, and when he came to me he already had $4 million in savings, with plenty of years to turn that into more. On a traditional financial path, an advisor would focus on growing that money. He'd probably end up with $10 million, all ready to leave to someone else. Without kids, it would go to his niece.

So I asked him, "What's your niece going to do with it?"

He said, "She'll be wealthy."

"No," I told him. "She's going to take that money and go live the life she wants, doing the things you didn't do with the money you earned. She's going to do the traveling you wanted to do. She's going to buy a new car you wanted to have. She's going to buy the house you never bought."

The truth is you can **either live a one-of-a-kind life, or you can leave your wealth behind to somebody else so they can have a one-of-a-kind life with your money.**

Not that there's anything wrong with that if it's what matters most to you—some people's one-of-a-kind life does involve leaving the biggest financial legacy possible. The point of the One of a Kind Financial Plan™ is for you to have the financial security to use your money the way you want.

For many of us, having a safety net for our children and leaving behind a legacy for them to have more opportunities is a big part of that, and that's great. There might be ways to do both. I want you to know that *you* also deserve a one-of-a-kind life—and that leaving *all* of your wealth behind isn't the *only* way to create a legacy.

You can create a legacy for your family and still live your one-of-a-kind life.

Maybe that means saving more for a while and growing your money strategically to support both. Maybe that means setting aside a certain amount for your family after you die and using everything else to support the life you want. Maybe it means adjusting your one-of-a-kind life (traveling on a smaller scale while still having amazing experiences or meeting new people or seeing new places). Maybe it means thinking about your legacy in an entirely different way, taking kids, nieces, nephews, parents, brothers, and sisters along for the ride, and experience life with you.

That's what we came up with for another of my clients, Jace, a 53-year-old divorcee with a set of 16-year-old twins. He came to me and said, "I've listened to your podcast and I know you're what I need. When my kids graduate next year, I want to go to Costa Rica and surf 320 days a year."

We looked at his assets; he had over a million in his retirement accounts and another million in home equity. He said, "I need to know how this money right here is going to let me surf 320 days. I'm not worried about what I leave behind. I want my kids to earn their wealth on their own."

Instead, we created a plan for Jace to pay for his kids to travel and visit him a few times a year, creating real "wow moments" together, moments that are going to be unlike anything else they've experienced in life.

He's going to do that for 4–5 years. What comes after that? He doesn't know yet. But whatever it is, he wants to really *experience* life. And the plan we created will make sure he gets to do that.

A traditional financial advisor might want Jace to take a different route, to work on growing that money more and more and to leave it behind. But Jace is a one-of-a-kind human—and he knew he needed a One of a Kind Financial Planner.

Another client, Sofia, is a ferociously independent 60-year-old woman. She was married once for just a few months, and she realized she never wanted to do that again. She never wanted to rely on anybody else's income. She never wanted to live with anybody again. But out of her relationship came a daughter, and eventually a granddaughter.

She does everything to be with them. To her, one-of-a-kind living means the ability to be invested in her granddaughter's life. But she also lives her own life, playing golf and enjoying the outdoors. She also organizes events for other seniors in her community to get outdoors, get active, and get healthy.

All of these people have unique, rich, full lives. And they needed an advisor to help them get the plan in place so they could enjoy those lives without the what-ifs and the fears and the uncertainty.

The One of a Kind Financial Plan™ is different because it:

- Starts at a different place
- Is created based on the life you want
- Is comprehensive and simple to implement
- Is about how much you've *lived* not how much you've earned
- Is driven by dreams—not by a number goal
- Teaches you to look at your money differently, your legacy differently, and your life differently

Before you move on, take a moment to ask yourself, what would you want to spend the next five years doing, if you had the financial plan in place to support it? It might not be 320 days of surfing in Costa Rica—but what would it be? Write down the answer.

Now…is that more exciting than writing down a goal number to hit? Or a percentage to save?

The One of a Kind Financial Plan™ focuses on doing things differently, solving the biggest financial challenges—like taxes, retirement income, and long-term care.

When you know you have the security, the flexibility, and the capability to really *live*, you get to stop worrying about the numbers and start your one-of-a-kind life. When you have the financial plan in place and the advice you need, there's nothing to hold you back.

If you're willing to think differently—and set aside the traditional rules—you can build something extraordinary. The One of a Kind Financial Plan™ will be there to support you as your life evolves.

Life is rarely a straight path. It's filled with unexpected twists, turns, and surprises. Sometimes those surprises are the best parts of the adventure. Sometimes they're challenges you didn't see coming. The key is to be prepared for whatever comes your way.

The One of a Kind Financial Plan™ creates that foundation. It's designed to be dynamic, to let you grow and adapt and pivot, like Jeff Bezos did. And it gives you clarity and confidence, so you can focus less on what might go wrong and more on what's possible.

What starts as a financial plan evolves into a life plan that grows with your dreams, and supports you every step of the way.

From here, we're going to move into Part 2 of this book where we start breaking down the nitty gritty of the One of a Kind Financial Plan™. But before we do, take a moment to remind yourself that this approach is different *for a reason*. You're going to be challenging advice you've heard along the way and learning a new, better approach. The journey isn't going to be what you imagined—but it will be worth it.

PART 2

This Is the Plan

CHAPTER 8

THE #1 THING YOU CAN DO TO TAKE CONTROL OF YOUR FINANCIAL FUTURE

"The best things in life are free, but sooner or later the government will find a way to tax them." —Anonymous

Sometimes clients ask me, "What's the best investment I can make?" My go-to response is a bit unexpected.

"A mattress," I tell them with a grin. It sounds like a joke, but the truth is that your money should be used to impact your life—and you spend more of your life in your bed than anywhere else.

But the answer goes in a different direction when people ask me, "What's the most important decision I can make with my money?"

It's easy to get fixated on investments. (After all, investing is where traditional financial advisors start—and where they put the vast majority of their focus.) But while investments are a key part of a financial plan, in the One of a Kind Financial Plan™, they aren't where we start. Why? Because they aren't what makes the *biggest* difference.

The thing that moves the needle more than anything else is *tax planning*, something that often gets overlooked in the traditional approach.

What you might not realize is that tax planning can:

- Drastically reduce the biggest expense you will face over your lifetime
- Create financial security that can't be achieved otherwise
- Protect you against the decisions the government might make in the future
- Free up secured money so you can invest it to create a multiplying effect

In this chapter, I'm going to reveal seven tax truths that show you *why* and *how* tax planning is the number one way to secure your financial future.

TAX TRUTH #1: TAXES ARE THE BIGGEST EXPENSE YOU PAY IN YOUR LIFE

Think about it—taxes are everywhere. It's not only federal taxes; there's state income tax for many people (and sometimes city tax as well). There's property tax, estate tax, and sales tax. You're paying taxes on essentially everything you own, and not always in small amounts.

At the federal level, income tax ranges from 10% to 37%.[2] Factor in other taxes, and some people are paying close to *half of their income* in taxes.

---

2 Internal Revenue Service. "Federal Income Tax Rates and Brackets." IRS.
gov. Accessed April 27, 2025. https://www.irs.gov/filing/federal-income-tax-rates-and-brackets.

When you add everything together, **taxes easily become the single largest expense in your lifetime.**

But we aren't being taught to think about controlling this expense. In fact, the common perception is that taxes are just something we can't do anything about. You earn money, taxes are taken out, and that's that. But this idea is a very costly myth.

In reality, you have more control over taxes than you think, which leads us to our second truth.

TAX TRUTH #2: YOU CHOOSE THE AMOUNT OF TAXES YOU PAY

What if I told you that you can control the amount of taxes you pay? You can't eliminate taxes altogether, but that doesn't mean you are helpless when it comes to taxes. You can control how much you pay.

We've all heard stories of billionaires paying next to nothing in taxes—and we think of them exploiting loopholes. But mitigating taxes is not about breaking the rules; it's about learning how to work within them. Think of tax planning as a financial game with its own set of rules, strategies, and potential for success.

Those billionaires? They've mastered the game. But the tax game isn't just reserved for billionaires. It's something everyone can, and should, learn how to play. The problem is, no one's teaching the rules to the general population.

We go to tax preparers and CPAs for help with taxes, meeting with them usually once a year to review what happened the year *before* (after it's too late to make any major difference). They're essentially historians, looking back on what's already happened, taking your documents and information, and putting everything into forms.

That doesn't mean they're doing anything wrong. They're doing their job, making sure your information is reported correctly. At the end of the day, though, they're just recording history.

Tax planning is different. It doesn't look back at what already happened. Tax planning is about looking ahead, making intentional choices today that will impact how much you'll pay in the future.

With proactive tax strategies, you can take control of how much you send to the IRS. And here's why this is more critical than ever...

TAX TRUTH #3: TAXES ARE LIKELY GOING TO GO UP IN THE FUTURE

We're living in a big, fragmented system of how to get money in retirement—but it hasn't always been that way. Until about 50 years ago, people essentially received a guaranteed monthly paycheck from pensions and Social Security payments.

Then came ERISA—the Employee Retirement Income Security Act, passed in 1974. This created IRAs (individual retirement accounts), and 401(k)s followed shortly with the Revenue Act in 1978. These accounts were positioned as a way to take control of retirement, especially for those without access to pension plans. The government also established them as tax-deferred, meaning the money isn't taxed when it goes into the account (it's taxed when it's withdrawn). We were told this was a tax break: *save the tax money now and you'll have more to invest/grow.* We've been told to defer taxes for decades since then. Americans have accumulated trillions of dollars in retirement accounts that have yet to be taxed.

401(k): An employer-sponsored retirement savings plan that allows employees to contribute a portion of their wages, often before taxes, to individual retirement accounts.

Individual Retirement Account (IRA): a tax-deferred personal retirement account.

The problem? That model was built on a theory that tax rates would be lower upon retirement—a theory that's false.

Taxes at the time of this writing are near historic lows. Meanwhile, the national debt continues to grow, expected to hit $54 trillion by 2033.[3] There are only two ways to balance that growing debt: reduce spending or increase taxes. Reduce spending is probably not going to happen at the levels needed to balance our budget and reduce debt. The reality is that we're likely heading into a future where tax rates increase.

David McKnight, author of *The Power of Zero*, highlighted the future of the American tax rate based on academic research. He predicted that the government is

---

3 Kanso, Sarah. "US government debt to top $54 trillion in next decade: CBO." ABC News, February 7, 2024. https://abcnews.go.com/Politics/us-government-debt-top-54-trillion-decade-cbo/story?id=107041188.

going to be insolvent (unable to pay their bills), likely within 20 years.[4] If this happens, tax hikes are almost inevitable.

(This isn't a matter of partisan politics, either. Politicians on both sides of the aisle promise lower tax rates. But it's important to remember that they are *politicians*. They're going to tell you what they know you want to hear now. But the truth is that we're going to hit a point in time when we spend so much more than what we bring in that even the best-intentioned politicians aren't going to realistically be able to stop tax rates from increasing.)

TAX TRUTH #4: DEFERRING TAXES DOESN'T SAVE YOU MONEY

Imagine that you're going to buy a house. You walk into a meeting at the bank about financing. They tell you they'll give you access to $750,000 today to buy the house. But they're not going to tell you what the interest will be until the end of the loan term—you have to agree to it without knowing. Would you take out that loan? Of course not. Yet that's exactly what's happening when we defer taxes into traditional retirement accounts year after year.

If taxes are expected to rise, deferring them becomes a gamble. When you defer taxes into the future, you're essentially saying, "I'll pay what the government decides to charge me later."

We've been told we're saving money when we defer taxes. And that idea feels very, very good. Who doesn't love a good deal? Who doesn't love feeling like we lowered our

---

4 McKnight, David. *The Power of Zero: How to Get to the 0% Tax Bracket and Transform Your Retirement*. Acanthus Publishing, 2014.

taxes? Tax breaks feel like power—almost like we've stuck it to the man.

But the truth is you aren't "saving" anything when you invest in tax-deferred accounts; you're simply delaying your taxes for retirement without knowing what the rates will be. What will the tax rates be in 30 years? Whatever the government decides…and we're just along for the ride.

Essentially, putting money in tax-deferred retirement assets like the 401(k) or traditional IRA is like making the government a business partner in your retirement account—a business partner that gets to decide how much they can take at any given time.

That's not to say that accounts like 401(k)s or IRAs are bad tools; they're not. But they're also not necessarily *the best for everyone*. There are some situations where tax-deferred plans make sense. For example, if you are leaving your money to someone who is in a significantly lower tax bracket than you. In this situation, it's a safe assumption that the overall tax burden will likely be higher if you pay taxes *now*. But this is the exception, not the rule. (That's the beauty of the One of a Kind Financial Plan™. It doesn't stick to one method or strategy for everyone. Tax planning is about taking a look at the big picture, including your taxes, the taxes of your beneficiaries, and what you can expect when you retire.)

In most cases, deferring taxes simply leaves you at the whim of the government. The government controls the taxes. The government controls the future. The government even gets to decide when and how much you have to take out of those accounts (also known as "required minimum distributions"). In other words, they get to tell you how much money you have to take out *and* at what level that money is taxed. You are at the mercy of whatever they decide—unless you make choices *now* that change that.

> **Required Minimum Distribution (RMD):** The minimum amount you must withdraw each year from your retirement accounts after reaching a certain age to satisfy tax rules.

TAX TRUTH #5: YOU CAN PROTECT YOUR MONEY AGAINST RISING TAXES

If you were to close this book today and walk away without ever coming back to it, I hope you take this one action—go out there and take a savvy approach to your taxes (one that protects your money against rising tax rates).

You don't have to let the government be that all-powerful business partner in your retirement. A lot has happened since the 1970s when these retirement accounts were first formed—and you have options and tools at your disposal that can change the game.

The simplest tool that many of you can put into play right away is taking advantage of Roth accounts. Roth IRAs and Roth 401(k)s allow you to grow your money tax-free after you've already paid taxes on the contributions.

> **Roth IRA:** A type of individual retirement account where you contribute after-tax dollars, eliminating taxes on your future earnings and qualified withdrawals.

This means the growth, withdrawals, and earnings are all yours. You won't be paying taxes on the income you take out. You won't be taxed on capital gains. You won't have to worry about rising tax rates. And you won't be wondering how much of your money is going to stay yours.

When you contribute or convert funds to a Roth, you effectively eliminate taxes on the growth forever and create tax-free income for the future. It also creates a tax-free inheritance for your beneficiaries. That's the REAL tax break (not deferring your taxes and hoping for the best rate somewhere down the line).

I've been doing this for a long time, and I've seen a lot of people come to me with buyer's remorse after doing what they've been told they're supposed to do by focusing on tax-deferred accounts. I've heard people share their biggest regrets.

I've never heard a single person say, "Man, I wish I would have put more money into my traditional accounts so I could pay more tax." But I've heard plenty say, "I wish I would have put more in my Roth sooner."

If you're reading this and thinking, "Uh-oh," I want you to know that it's not your fault. You've done what you've been told to do. You've followed the advice and leadership you thought you were supposed to. And if you've been led astray, I'm sorry. You're in the same boat as millions of other people. But you don't have to stay on that boat.

TAX TRUTH #6: BIG COMPANIES AREN'T INCENTIVIZED TO TELL YOU ANY OF THIS

If everything I have told you is true, why isn't this talked about more? Why isn't every financial professional out there telling their clients to max out Roth accounts and start creating tax-free income in retirement?

To answer that question, follow the money. I'm not here to tell you that financial companies are the boogeyman out to get you. But I do want you to think very carefully about how the financial professionals that handle your money are compensated.

The financial industry isn't motivated to help you plan for taxes. Why? Because it's not in their financial interest. Firms that manage your retirement accounts earn fees based on the total value of your assets. If you choose to reduce the balance of those accounts by paying taxes now, through something like a Roth conversion, they make less money.

For example, if you have $1 million in a traditional 401(k), a financial advisor might manage all $1 million. If you convert $300,000 to a Roth IRA and pay taxes upfront, your account balance drops, and so does the advisor's fee. They're making 30% less money off of you.

But if you don't do what I've talked about in this chapter, if you don't take action and get tax savvy, there's more money invested in the market. That creates a conflict of interest where advisors might not encourage strategies that are ultimately better for you.

This is why they don't offer anything like the One of a Kind Financial Plan™ and why tax planning is not a focus for many big name companies.

TAX TRUTH #7: TAX PLANNING CREATES CERTAINTY

Tax planning isn't a magic button. It's not a sleazy get-rich-quick-scheme or a flash-in-the-pan investment.

It's a control mechanism. None of us know what the future holds. We might have medical expenses or unexpected situations that force us to retire early or any number of things that we can't completely account for.

There's so much about retirement we can't be certain about. There's so much about *life* we can't be certain about. But we do know that no matter what comes our way, taxes are a certainty—the largest expense we'll ever have.

Tax planning is how you take some control of what happens to your money in the future. And it's how you take control over what you *can* so that you live your one-of-a-kind life for as long as you can.

That's what the One of a Kind Financial Plan™ is really all about: putting you in the driver's seat so you can be as certain as possible in an uncertain world, so you gain as much security as you can and as much freedom to live the life you want.

> *The One of a Kind Financial Plan™ is all about putting you in the driver's seat so you can be as certain as possible in an uncertain world.*

No matter how long you've been led astray or how much bad advice you've received in the past, you get to make a change now. You get to know better. You get to do better. And you get to choose a better journey for yourself.

CHAPTER 9

THE 5 STEPS FOR A ONE OF A KIND FINANCIAL PLAN™

Now that you understand why an individualized plan needs to begin with your one-of-a-kind life in mind, it's time to break down what actually goes into a One of a Kind Financial Plan™.

In this chapter, I'm going to break down the five core steps: tax planning, income planning, investment management, long-term care, and legacy planning. I'll explain how my approach to each differs from traditional financial planning.

STEP 1: TAX PLANNING

I covered tax planning in Chapter 8 because it's the foundation of the One of a Kind Financial Plan™.

Tax planning takes your real-life, present data, and asks: In the next year, and beyond, how can we reduce your lifetime taxes? How can we position your assets so they're never taxed again? And how can we eventually get you out of the tax system altogether, so future increases don't touch you?

You already learned that taxes are the single largest expense you'll face in your lifetime. This doesn't end just because you retire; they remain your biggest financial obligation. **That's why the biggest return on investment you can ever have is getting yourself in a tax neutral or tax free position.**

Remember, the traditional financial standpoint—the theory that you'll have a lower tax rate in retirement—is a myth. Even if you believe that taxes won't go up, to have a lower tax rate in retirement, you will need to substantially reduce your income in retirement.

This is where the old idea of the "80% rule" comes from (traditional advice that tells you to plan to live on 80% of your current income after you retire). I don't know about you, but I don't want to work for decades just to live life at 80% after I retire. I want 100% of the life I worked to create.

Most people don't want to downgrade their lifestyle in retirement—they want to maintain or upgrade it. And maintaining the same quality of life means staying in the same tax bracket, unless you do the planning necessary to have lower taxes.

This is why unlike traditional financial advising (which often overlooks tax planning entirely), this step comes first in the One of a Kind Financial Plan™. It controls your biggest expense, provides the greatest return on investment, and ensures that your future isn't dictated by outdated, one-size-fits-all advice. **Instead of living 80% of your dreams, you can plan for 100% of the lifestyle you deserve, without compromise.**

A One of a Kind Financial Plan™ in Action:

My client, Eric, was 75 years old, with $2.6 million sitting in an IRA (individual retirement account).

He was looking for tax planning support. But even reaching out to professionals who "specialize" in tax planning didn't bring Eric the results he needed. He kept hearing the same advice over and over: "Convert that money to a Roth IRA." These professionals knew the tax truths that I shared in Chapter 8. They knew the benefits of paying taxes now instead of deferring them into the future. But they weren't looking at the big picture, and they also weren't explaining *why* he should do that.

When I met with Eric, I asked him not just about his current tax bracket, but also his children's.

Eric was in the oil industry, and his income fell into the 32% tax bracket. His only beneficiaries were his two children. They were going to inherit his wealth. But one of them was a personal trainer, and the other worked in retail. They both fell in the 12% tax bracket.

If he converted his money at the age of 75, he would end up paying significantly more in taxes than his children would when they inherited the money.

Roth conversions are a great tool for so many people— they're something I recommend for many of my clients. But like I pointed out in Chapter 8, they aren't always the answer.

This is why it's so important to take a comprehensive, individual approach to financial planning. Tax planning is really about lifetime family taxes. For many people, Roth conversions make sense; their children will be better off than them, so paying the taxes early is often better. But for people in Eric's situation, converting funds to Roth accounts isn't the best choice. In his case, smart tax planning meant leaving his money in tax-deferred accounts, knowing that his children would be in a lower tax bracket.

Eric told me that he spoke with eight different people. Every one of them told him to do Roth conversions. I was the first person that gave him different advice, but I was also the first person that bothered to explain the rationale. The other advisors didn't even ask about the tax brackets of his beneficiaries—they just stuck to a one-size-fits-all approach.

STEP 2: INCOME PLANNING

Step 1 offers the most control and the biggest return on investment (ROI) for your finances, but Step 2 addresses the biggest fear that most people have in retirement—running out of money.

When you're working, running out of money is rarely a thought. Even if you lose your job, you think, "I'll find another one." It might be inconvenient, but you know it's temporary. Retirement doesn't work that way. Stepping into retirement means voluntarily leaving the workforce, and with that comes the fear of not having enough money to last.

That fear makes sense. During your working years, you're used to getting regular paychecks every two weeks or every month. You've built an entire life around that steady, predictable income. But when you retire, that rhythm changes, and most people don't know how to transition from an employee paycheck model to a retirement paycheck model.

No one teaches you how to make that shift. For decades, you've been told to save, save, save. But once you've saved all that money, the question becomes, "Now what? How do I use it?"

Most people think of their retirement savings as assets. What they don't realize is that those assets need to be used to *buy retirement income.*

Retirement income is the money you have to support yourself in retirement; it's the money that you will either receive or withdraw each month to meet your expenses. For many people, Social Security makes up part of this income, but Social Security alone isn't enough for most people to live on. In fact, it's designed to make up about 40% of the retirement income the average person needs.[5]

Pension plans are another form of retirement income. These are employer-funded accounts that pay out monthly in retirement. While these were once a core part of most retirement income, they're more rare now. (In Chapter 8, I discussed how 401(k)s came to replace pension plans.) Now, pension plans are typically limited to unionized workers in the public sector, such as teachers or firefighters or military workers with 20 years of service. Some private companies offer pension plans, but if you have one, you're in the minority.

So if Social Security alone isn't enough, and you don't have a pension, that means you have to *create your*

---

5   https://www.ssa.gov/newsletter/Statement%20Insert%2025+.pdf

retirement income. Pension plan replacements such as 401(k)s, IRAs, and Roth IRAs, are a common way to do this. That's what retirement savings accounts were always meant for—they're not only to "save" money for retirement, they're to create reliable income in retirement. Put simply, when you contribute to a retirement account, you're putting aside money that you can later withdraw as part of your retirement income strategy.

Retirement savings accounts aren't the only option for retirement income. There are two types of retirement income you can create: variable income (money that can fluctuate with the stock market) and guaranteed income (money that is designated, fixed, and not dependent on the stock market).

Variable income options can include stocks, mutual funds, some types of life insurance policies, and brokerage accounts. In addition to pensions and Social Security, guaranteed retirement income can include bonds, annuities, and other types of life insurance policies.

> Bonds: Fixed-income investments where you lend money to an entity, like a government or corporation, in exchange for regular interest payments and the return of the principal amount at a set date.

Traditional advisors often don't focus on retirement income at all. They jump right into investment management because they are often only licensed to sell one or few options. They focus on "save and invest" instead of creating secure income.

But the truth is that most people benefit from a balance of retirement income—they need both certainty and security for the future as well as the opportunity to grow money through investments.

In the One of a Kind Financial Plan™, we determine what makes sense for you based on where you are now and where you need to be, then build stable guaranteed income to eliminate the fear of running out of money and make sure that you have enough to sustain the life you've built. (Only then do we move on to investment management.)

A One of a Kind Financial Plan™ in Action:
We recently worked with a couple, Cynthia and Frederick. They're 60 and 67 years old, married with no children, and facing the unique complexities of the retirement landscape. Frederick worked a steady federal job for three decades, while Cynthia ran a private practice for 20 years.

Together, they had saved over a million dollars, including an inheritance, thinking they were doing all the right things. But they just recently discovered minimum distribution requirements, the minimum amount they were going to withdraw from Frederick's retirement accounts based on his age. These withdrawals would push their tax burden higher just as they began living on a combination of that income, a pension, and Social Security.

Cynthia and Frederick had lived their whole lives sacrificing and saving. They put off home repairs. They still had a mortgage on their home. And they had traveled only on small budgets, focused on saving.

They told me that they would love to travel but, like most people in their age bracket, their biggest fear was running out of money.

With no children to leave assets to, they want to focus on living a full life. But without proper planning, they were worried about running into financial trouble at a time when they should be enjoying retirement most.

It took two hours to draw out their dreams, fears, stress points, and questions—all the things that make planning personal. This is why the One of a Kind Financial Plan™ (created with a One of a Kind Financial Planner) is different.

After working through all of their fears, their desires, and the life they wanted, I was able to show Cynthia and Frederick that they had been saving and hoarding their money with no purpose. We were able to establish a clear plan for their retirement income and document everything so that they could ease the stress and the worry. We made sure that they were able to withdraw what they needed every month to cover their expenses. We also designated funds for the home repair projects they wanted to handle. Once their fears were addressed by securing up their income, they were able to go out and focus on enjoying the time they earned after all of their hard work.

When they first told me that they wanted to travel, I asked them what the biggest trip on their bucket list was. They told me they wanted to go to Albuquerque, New Mexico.

Now, Albuquerque is a great city. It's a wonderful place to visit, full of food and culture. But that was the *biggest* that Cynthia and Frederick would allow themselves to imagine. I encouraged them to think bigger and dream bigger, beyond a small trip. Now that their One of a Kind Financial Plan™ is in place, they're able to see that they can do so much more.

They recently traveled to Colombia. They're preparing for a two-week trip to Ireland, Scotland, and England—a trip that connects to their heritage. And they're planning ahead for a trip to Italy and Greece in the near future.

That's the power of a One of a Kind Financial Plan™. It shows you how to look at your finances differently. It creates security. And it empowers you to use your money to think bigger and do things you never allowed yourself to imagine.

STEP 3: INVESTMENT MANAGEMENT

Investment management is where traditional financial planning *starts*, but in the One of a Kind Financial Plan™, it's right in the middle of the 5 steps. Why? Because I firmly believe it's impossible to create a truly effective investment strategy without first solving for taxes and retirement income.

If you haven't solved for taxes or ensured that you aren't going to run out of money, how can you possibly jump into investments? How could you determine the right investment strategy? It doesn't make sense. That's why we place it in the middle—not at the start.

The first piece to understand about investment management is that saving is not the same as investing. Saving is about putting money away, while investing is about creating growth and building wealth based on your specific situation, the life you're working toward, your needs, and your risk tolerance (how you're going to react if the value of your accounts goes down due to market fluctuation; I'll go into this more in Chapter 10).

The second piece to understand is that there is something more important than your *"return OF investment"* (ROI). Your ROI means how much money is added from growth when compared to how much money you invest. This is a key focus of the one-size-fits-all approach. But the One of a Kind Financial Plan™ focuses more on your *return OF investment*…meaning, when you invest money you earned through your hard work, your time, and your energy, you should be getting back freedom, time, energy, and most importantly, enjoyment of your life.

Your investment strategy should focus on giving you the life you want. It should also focus on investing in things that align with your values and that feel right to you. And that requires a financial planner who talks to you, understands what matters to you, and *educates* you on where they're putting your money and why.

Unfortunately, the traditional approach tends to skip the education piece. They'll tell you that the strategy *they* chose *for you* is "set it and forget it." But that leaves you fully putting your financial future in someone else's hands.

Don't get me wrong—it's important to have someone professionally manage your money. But that someone should make sure you have a baseline understanding of your investments and your financial strategy.

The One of a Kind Financial Plan™ empowers you to understand investments that work for you, connecting the dots between where you are now and where you want to go. Basic financial education is part of the process. We want you to know that your investment strategy has a purpose, and that the tools you use for investment—and the risk you take—can and should change throughout your life.

Think of it like climbing a mountain. The tools you use, the gear you bring, even the muscles you need to train to get up to the top of a mountain aren't the same as the ones you use coming down. The same thing you do pre-retirement to build up more money isn't the same thing you do in retirement: the way you save, the investments, the risk you tolerate—they're different. Unfortunately most investment advisors say to use the same tools for both; that's their status quo. **But a One of a Kind Financial Plan™ understands that the tools you use to go up the mountain are different from the ones you need to go down.**

That's why the One of a Kind Financial Plan™ is created to be dynamic. We might move your investments around based on risk at a certain point in your life and make changes along the way. But the big difference is that you aren't left in the dark, blindly hoping we have your best interests at heart. We're updating you, educating you, empowering you, and inviting you to be a part of the decision-making process (with a One of a Kind Financial Planner who can explain the purpose behind the decisions we recommend).

A ONE OF A KIND FINANCIAL PLAN™ IN ACTION

My client, Seth, was referred to me by another financial professional. Seth is 55 years old with a nice nest egg in progress: He and his wife had combined investments worth about $3.6 million. They are both first-generation wealth, coming from nothing. The more they have grown their wealth, the more they have wanted to know about their money—what they're invested in, where their money is going, and most importantly, *why* it's going there.

Unfortunately, they never got the answers they were looking for. They were simply told they needed to invest and grow their wealth. But Seth felt that he had no *purpose* with his money. He also experienced underlying fears about running out of money or making the wrong choices with his investments.

So when I met with him, I explained how the One of a Kind Financial Plan™ works, taking each step and putting it toward the vision for his one-of-a-kind life. I taught him that aligning his investments with his purpose in life was far more important than the execution of individual stocks, bonds, or annuities. I told him that the purpose of investing money wasn't to build the biggest account; it was to provide freedom to live the life he wanted.

For the first time, Seth could understand the purpose of investing and growing his money. He told me, "I have finally found my financial planner."

As we created his One of a Kind Financial Plan™, Seth gained the peace and comfort of knowing that he was not going to leave too much or too little money to his three kids when he passed away. He was also able to feel secure knowing that he and his wife could retire early and live for a good part of their lives traveling and doing the things they enjoyed. His fears and worries were gone, and he finally saw the opportunities his money could create.

STEP 4: LONG-TERM CARE

Planning for long-term care isn't the most exciting topic, but it's one of the most important topics.

What happens if you face medical challenges? What happens if you can't take care of yourself? What happens if you end up with dementia? (Many people would say, "I never want to live like that." But when you're actually in it, it's different. My grandmother struggled with dementia for 15 years. Not once did she say she wanted her life to end. You need to create a plan for how you'll pay for care when you need it.)

You can't predict everything, but you'll need to plan for how you're going to be cared for *without becoming a financial burden to your loved ones.*

Long-term care planning focuses on answering questions like:

1. *What kind of care do I want when I can no longer care for myself?*
2. *How important is my independence to me? Do I want to be in a nursing home? An assisted living facility? Or have a caregiver come to my home if possible?*
3. *How likely am I to face medical issues? Will I be able to cover those expenses if they arrive?*

Long-term care costs can add up quickly. The *median* cost per year for a private room in a nursing home is $116,800 (meaning for a top-tier facility or in an area with high cost of living, you'll likely pay more). For a semi-private room, it's $104,025. To have someone come into your home, it's between $68,000-$75,000. An assisted living facility costs a median of $64,200.[6] And all of those prices are only likely to go up if the cost of living rises over time.

That's a lot of money that needs to be designated and set aside. Part of long-term care planning is ensuring you have enough money to cover emergency expenses and health insurance. But it can also involve self-funding the type of care you want through health savings accounts or purchasing long-term care insurance that covers expenses that health insurance doesn't.

The unfortunate truth is that if you don't create a long-term care plan, your loved ones are going to bear these costs—and if they can't afford the option you would prefer, your life is going to be out of your control.

The only person you can truly rely on to take care of your older self is your younger self. By addressing long-term care now, you're creating a safety net that ensures dignity, independence, and security during later years. You're also ensuring that you're not a burden to those who care about you.

Once again, traditional financial advisors often don't discuss these options with you because they might not be licensed in these areas. They might be able to refer you to someone else or answer some of your questions if *you* bring them up, but they aren't proactively guiding you through this process or asking the questions that really need to be asked.

But One of a Kind Financial Planners know that your financial future can't be piecemealed: long-term care is a

---

6 https://www.statista.com/statistics/310446/annual-median-rate-of-long-term-care-services-in-the-us/

key part of your one-of-a-kind life, and it has to be part of your financial plan.

A One of a Kind Financial Plan™ in Action:
One of my clients, Paula, is a 67-year-old woman who recently met the love of her life—a 48-year-old man. After four years together, they are engaged and planning their wedding. It's going to be a magical time. Her life is definitely one of a kind.

Paula is first-generation wealth. She grew up poor but has followed the traditional path of saving and working hard. In her 30s and 40s, she spent a decade overseas, experiencing life, broadening her horizons, meeting people, and finding herself. When she came back, she started focusing on saving and did some real estate investing. Paula is smart. She's driven. She's a hard worker. And she tried to go the do-it-yourself route. But all she has ever discovered is one-size-fits-all advice.

She came to me because she was ready to do things differently. After all, she knew her life was anything but cookie-cutter.

When I first met with Paula, I asked her what her earliest memory was relating to money. She told me that it was her first job as a teenager, where she learned about earning and saving her own money. What I didn't know at the time was that she was holding something back.

It wasn't until a few meetings later that Paula told me, "Remember when you asked me what my earliest memory of money was? I'd like to change my answer. When you asked me that, I didn't know if I was going to stick with you or not, so I didn't want to tell you the whole truth. Now I know."

Paula went on to tell me that her actual earliest memory of money was coming home from school as a child and being sent straight to bed. Her parents couldn't afford to feed her dinner, so they would put her to bed early.

She told me, "That's why I've saved my money. So I would never have to be hungry again."

It's heartbreaking to think about, but it's a story with a happy ending. She promised herself and worked hard to make sure she would never go hungry again. She worked for years—and now we've created a financial plan to give her the security to know she never will. As a result, she gets to live out the rest of her life with confidence that she can enjoy her time with her future husband and not have to worry about finances.

With the age gap in their marriage, one of the biggest pieces we focused on is long-term care. Paula wants as much time as possible with the love of her life. In fact, she told me her goal is to live beyond 100! But she also wants to make sure that her long-term care is planned and provided for so that when the time comes, when she can't care for herself anymore, and her husband is dealing with the grief and emotions that will come, he won't also be having to scramble financially to figure out how to care for her. Everything will be planned, in place, and documented, so that they can live their one-of-a-kind lives together in peace as long as possible.

STEP 5: LEGACY PLANNING

Do you have a will? If so, you're in the minority. Roughly 76% of Americans don't have a will and a trust.[7]

But here's the reality. If you don't have a will, your state government has written one for you. Probate rules will dictate how your assets get divided—and your loved ones will end up coping with stress, delays, and legalities. In fact, the average probate court process takes 6–12 months.[8] It is also a public record for anyone to search and see into your past life. A will can drastically speed up the process, taking only a few months. A will also ensures that everything is handled privately, not on public record.

Legacy planning means that you have an individualized plan for who cares for your minor children, who gets your assets, and how to divide up things like land or complicated assets. A customized legacy plan also communicates your wishes for your own health status and long-term care, as well as your funeral arrangements. In short, it ensures that your wishes for your family and assets are respected.

But legacy planning doesn't only involve creating a will. It also involves creating a trust—a way to hold your wealth until a specific time or when your children reach a certain age. This can help you determine how and when your money is given to beneficiaries instead of leaving everything in one lump sum. This can help make sure that the money isn't used irresponsibly (especially important with younger beneficiaries who are more likely to spend their inheritance than save and invest).

---

7   https://www.caring.com/caregivers/estate-planning/wills-survey/

8   https://www.legalzoom.com/articles/how-long-does-probate-take

Funds placed in a trust also avoid probate, meaning your loved ones will have access to assets faster, without everything being tied up with red tape.

A trust can even ease the tax burden left behind on your loved ones. Estate taxes can range from 18% to 40% depending on the value of what you leave behind.[9] But when you transfer money from your estate into *trusts* you can reduce the taxable amount using lifetime credits and exemptions.

What most people don't realize is that trusts are not only for what happens to your money after you die; they're also in place to provide financial planning for your long-term care while you're still alive. With a trust in place, your family members can effectively pay bills and manage money while you're still living to reduce the financial burden of your care.

This is why a legacy plan matters so much. It's far more than avoiding probate or administration concerns. When your legacy is well-planned, it becomes a love letter to those you care about. Remember, legacy is about so much more than a number left behind. Your assets are not your legacy— *you* are your legacy: the stories your loved ones share about you, the impact you left on your community, what you stood for, how you lived your life, how people remember you. All of these pieces go into the discussion of legacy planning in the One of a Kind Financial Plan™.

> *When your legacy is well-planned, it becomes a love letter to those you care about.*

9 https://www.cnbc.com/select/what-is-estate-tax-and-who-pays-it/

A One of a Kind Financial Plan™ in Action

Some of my earliest clients were a couple named Paul and Josephine Stetson. This sweet older couple from New York had a son who grew up to become a successful doctor.

Eventually, they reached the age where they could no longer keep up with paying bills or organizing their finances.

Fortunately, we had planned ahead for this moment, establishing the Stetson Family Trust. This became the foundation that allowed their son, Dr. William, to handle their bills and finances while also running a major medical practice.

Dr. William was able to use a checkbook tied to the trust to pay his parents' mortgage and utilities every month so that everything was handled on time. He was also able to use the funds to pay for a nurse to visit his parents regularly, making sure they were healthy and cared for.

Without the trust in place, Dr. William would have had to navigate administration issues, try to figure out how to access accounts and transfer money to cover costs, or have to bear the financial burden himself, all while trying to focus on his career.

This happened before online bill pay or iPhones—but even with those technological changes, admin issues aren't always accounted for. It can be difficult to figure out passwords, log in to accounts, and navigate online banking when cognitive decline is in the picture. But a trust is a document that has stood the test of time. It allows families to care for each other no matter what technology comes or how fast things change.

BRINGING IT ALL TOGETHER

There are a lot of components within the One of a Kind Financial Plan™, and that might seem intimidating. But you'll notice that many of the tools involved in each of these steps are things you've probably heard of, even if you've never been truly educated on what they entail or how they work.

The One of a Kind Financial Plan™ isn't trying to lead you into anything sketchy or untested. It brings together practical solutions, academic knowledge, Wall Street expertise and 100 years of historical knowledge.

A One of a Kind Financial Plan™ is personalized, but it's still likely to share *some* overlapping features with other people's plans. You might be invested in similar products or use a similar tax approach. But YOU are what makes it different.

The uniqueness appears around the edges, where it matters most. How can your funds be put to the best use? What is the best tax strategy for you? What level of protection do you need? Do your loved ones rely on your income—and if so, how can you provide for them after you're gone? How much risk can you afford to take? What are you missing out on if you don't take on risk?

A traditional financial advisor will mainly focus on investment management depending on which products they're licensed to sell. They're not going to give you the full toolbox. Some of the pieces, like *tax planning*, they won't even touch. (Think back to the burger joint problem from Chapter 5.) They're often trained to think what they're licensed to do is the one and only best way to do things.

They'll send you to a CPA for your taxes, or an attorney for your will, pushing you right into the Piecemeal Effect I talked about in Chapter 6.

And maybe, just maybe, if you connect with enough different people (and you educate yourself enough on all of the available options), you can hit all of these steps even while working with a traditional financial advisor.

But why wouldn't you want to use a plan that brings it all together? Why wouldn't you want to take a comprehensive approach?

Think of it like working with a personal trainer. You wouldn't go to one person for cardio, another for strength training, and yet another for nutrition, when you could have an expert create a plan specifically for you and guide you through the entire process.

With the One of a Kind Financial Plan™, you have one advisor who understands you, your priorities, and your concerns. There's no bouncing between professionals; no logging into apps trying to figure out what you've been invested in; no juggling appointments; no moving documents back and forth between people; and no extra work falling back on you to piece it all together. Everything is streamlined, connected, and created just for you.

Creating Your One of a Kind Financial Plan™

I want you to have a simple roadmap to follow. I want you to be educated on each piece, but I also want to make the complex simple and keep the heavy lifting on us instead of you.

In the One of a Kind Financial Plan™, everything's laid out. Everything's clear. Everything's in place. And you can call your financial planner if you have any questions or if anything changes—a person who really *knows* you.

That's what really matters, because the real power of the One of a Kind Financial Plan™ lies in how it takes into account the human side of finances. It's not just about crunching numbers. It's about weaving together the whole picture. The dream life. The fears. The worries. The stressors. The dynamics.

And that's what sets the plan apart. It answers the essential question, "Why is money important to me?" It helps you define what makes you one of a kind and creates a roadmap that takes you from worrying about money to living without fear of it. The five components of the plan work together to solve for the uncertainties, like stress, fears, and what-ifs, so you can finally take control of your financial future.

Once your plan is in place, you're free to live your one-of-a-kind life.

THE BIGGEST TAKEAWAYS

I know we've covered a lot in this chapter, and it can feel overwhelming. So let's make sure you walk away with the three most important pieces:

1. Being educated about finances is far more important than just trusting your advisor. You're the one who has to live with whatever the outcome is. You're the one who is going to be living this every single day. You need to be actively participating in the plan.
2. There are a lot of uncertainties in life, and the best we can do is control what we can control. The good news

is there is a lot we can do—we can control the amount of taxes we pay, we can control the fear of running out of money, we can control our risk, we can control not being a burden, and we can control the legacy we leave behind.

3. You don't have to do the one-size-fits-all plan. Your investment strategy, your tax strategy, and your retirement income strategy are about *you*. It's about your life. It's not about an advisor's life. It's not about a corporation's bottom line. It's not about the profitability of Wall Street or the Pro or how much your advisor makes in income. It's about using your money to get the one-of-a-kind life you want and deserve.

CHAPTER 10

WHAT TO KNOW FIRST

Now that you understand the structure of the One of a Kind Financial Plan™, it's time to look at the factors that you need to assess, clarify, and address before you start creating yours.

EVALUATING YOUR DEBT

The first area where you need to get clear is understanding your personal debt situation.

One of the biggest myths I see from online gurus is that your number one focus should be on paying off all of your debt. So many people think they can't even begin saving or investing until they are 100% debt free.

The truth is, you don't have to wait to be debt-free before working toward your one-of-a-kind life. But, you *do* need to have your debt under control.

Debt can do one of two things: It can be a powerful tool for growing wealth, or it can rob you of your future because you are paying for past indulgences with your current income. And the difference comes down to controllable or uncontrolled debt.

Uncontrolled debt might be mounting credit card balances, personal loans taken out to pay off other loans, or constantly relying on home equity lines of credit without a clear plan to pay them back. This type of debt is a roadblock you need to work through before you're ready for a One of a Kind Financial Plan™.

Controllable debt, on the other hand, is manageable and can even work in your favor. Fixed-rate mortgages, for example, allow you to own a home while keeping payments predictable. Business debt can help fund and grow a profitable venture when it's tied to a stable source of income and a clear plan to repay it.

The key here is ensuring that you're in control of how and when your debt is going to be paid off.

If your debt is controlled, you can build that into your plan and keep moving forward. But if your debt is out of control right now, that's where your focus should be. Work toward stabilizing it, creating a payoff plan, or tackling high-interest balances so you can regain control. Then, you can start your One of a Kind Financial Plan™. (And if you need help getting your debt under control, visit mikemilligan. com and request to speak to a financial coach about your debt.)

UNRESOLVED TAX ISSUES

If you owe money to the IRS or are in the process of sorting out tax issues, it's important to acknowledge how this can complicate building your financial plan. Tax-related problems don't mean you can't start planning for your future, but they do need to be addressed to create a truly effective and stress-free roadmap.

To move forward, it's essential to develop a clear strategy for handling your tax obligations, whether that means negotiating a payment plan with the IRS or addressing overdue filings. The sooner these issues are resolved, the sooner you can fully dedicate your energy to your One of a Kind Financial Plan™.

GAUGE YOUR FINANCIAL LITERACY

If there's still a lot you don't know about the pieces of the One of a Kind Financial Plan™ we covered in the last chapter, that's okay. It's not your fault—nobody's been teaching you what you need to know. But building financial literacy (the ability to understand your finances and make informed decisions with your money) is going to be part of the process for a successful plan.

Understanding what you already know (and what you don't know) will help you seek the knowledge you need to build. When you know more, you can do more, and that confidence affects everything from day-to-day decisions to long-term strategies.

A One of a Kind Financial Planner will make the complex simple and help you get the knowledge you need to be an active participant in your plan.

UNDERSTANDING YOUR RISK

Knowing your personal risk tolerance is another important piece of the puzzle. How are you going to emotionally react to things you can't control? Are you going to be able to stick to the plan and still sleep at night?

Risk is part of life—it's there. We can't control it. That's why it's important to control what you *can* control and build a plan that takes risk into account.

Most people think that risk is just the up and down of the market. But market risk is just one of the risk factors that go into financial planning. There are other risks.

- Tax Risk: The possibility of taxes rising unexpectedly, which could reduce your income and impact your financial goals.
- Longevity Risk: Living longer than expected and potentially running out of money later in life.
- Mortality Risk: The financial challenges of dying sooner than planned, especially if someone else relies on your income.
- Inflation Risk: The rising cost of living impacting your future.
- Liquidity Risk: Not having enough readily available cash for emergencies or unexpected needs.

It might sound like a lot but there are two great ways to manage those risks: building your financial literacy and working with a trusted financial professional who can help you stick to your plan.

History shows us, time and again, that people without a plan or advisor are more likely to panic, whether it's during a market downturn or another type of financial shock. That kind of emotional response can have lasting consequences. Take the 2008 financial crisis: many people panicked, pulled out of the market, and missed the market's eventual recovery, ultimately losing out on significant future wealth.

The good news is, risks don't have to mean roadblocks. There are solutions to address each type of risk. For instance:

- Tax risk: Roth conversions, if right for you, can help reduce your taxable income in future years.
- Longevity risk: Planning for retirement income can help mitigate the risk of running out of money, and creating a long-term care policy can account for potential health situations.
- Mortality risk: Life insurance policies can make sure those who depend on your income are protected.
- Inflation risk: When you have enough long-term money invested you can rest assured that your gains will be greater than the cost of rising prices.
- Liquidity risk: When you plan for the unexpected and create an established emergency fund, you don't have to worry that unforeseen expenses will derail your life in retirement.

> *The One of a Kind Financial Plan™ is how you reduce risk by controlling what you can control so you're secure about what you can't.*

The answer to risk isn't to avoid investing or to just save more money. In fact, the One of a Kind Financial Plan™ is how you *reduce risk* by controlling what you can control so you're secure about what you can't.

OVERCOMING THE PAST

Many people hesitate to work with a financial advisor or planner because they've been led astray in the past. It's easy to carry that frustration forward and decide, "Never again." But here's the thing—a bad teacher doesn't mean you quit school, and a bad meal doesn't mean you stop eating. A single bad fit doesn't mean professional financial planning, as a whole, isn't for you.

Bad experiences are just part of your financial story— but you get to decide what gets written next. Tony Robbins once said, "The secret to success is to learn to use pain and pleasure instead of having pain and pleasure use you."[10] This wisdom applies here. Instead of letting a bad experience with a financial professional hold you back or dictate your future, you can choose to learn from it and move forward.

GETTING CLEAR ABOUT WHAT MATTERS MOST

Effective financial planning starts with one essential question—what truly matters most to you? Without clarity on your values and priorities, it's easy to get distracted by the wrong strategies.

For example, we worked with a client who initially told us her one-of-a-kind life was about extensive travel in retirement. But seven months later, she asked to dip into funds we had set aside for those future adventures.

I reminded her of our plan and let her know that if we took out that money it would affect the future. She said, "I

---

10 Robbins, Tony. "Pillars for An Extraordinary Life." X, November 16, 2017, 10:19 AM, https://x.com/TonyRobbins/status/931263258417250304.

know, but spoiling my grandkids on Christmas morning is more important to me than a vacation five years from now. I want to create a magical morning for them."

So I said, "Let's do it." We made the changes in the plan and moved in the new direction of what mattered the most to her.

A one-of-a-kind life means focusing on the things that are the most important, knowing that there are other things you might not be able to achieve or accomplish or do. You have to understand how your choices today impact what you're doing tomorrow.

Paula Pant, host of the Afford Anything podcast, says, "You can afford anything, but not everything."[11] That quote captures the heart of financial planning. You can't do it all, but you can do what matters most. And when you understand what those priorities are, you're no longer just making a plan—you're building your one-of-a-kind life.

11 Pant, Paula. *Afford Anything*. Afford Anything LLC. https://affordanything.com/podcast/.

PART 3

This Is the Process

CHAPTER 11

BUILD YOUR VISION

You've learned a lot in this book, from the intricacies of tax planning and the importance of creating retirement income, to how different advisors operate and the distinction between controlled debt and uncontrolled debt. Now it's time to learn how to put those lessons into play to create a financial plan that lets you make your dream life a reality. In the rest of this book, I'm going to walk you through the first steps you need to take, including how to define your vision, how to find the right professionals to make it happen, and how to strengthen your financial literacy so you can make informed decisions along the way.

The most important thing to remember is that you need to start by creating your vision for your one-of-a-kind life. Getting clear on the vision matters—remember, without the vision, your plan isn't taking you anywhere.

To set the stage, I want to share a story with you of someone who put together a powerful vision with the plan to get him there—Steve Jobs. It's hard to think of anybody more revolutionary, but there was a time when Jobs wasn't on the path to becoming the trailblazer we think of today.

He struggled in school, dropped out of college, and seemed aimless.

He was intelligent; there's no denying that. But he didn't have anywhere to channel his brilliance. He didn't have anything driving him toward something big.

In 1974, that changed. Jobs left his job at Atari and embarked on a journey to India to "find himself." He studied Eastern philosophy, spent time with monks, and questioned where he was heading with his life. And in the process, he learned a lot about himself—what he wanted and what he didn't want.

When he returned seven months later, he was a changed man. He didn't come back with new technical skills or business secrets. He came back with something more important: *a vision*.

That vision was to make an impact in the world, or in his words, "put a ding in the universe." And that's exactly what he set out to do. Jobs co-founded Apple in his family's garage with Steve Wozniak, and the rest is quite literally history. He changed the world. He put a ding in the universe. He became arguably the most famous tech person of all time—a symbol of pioneering, advancement, and innovation.

We can learn a lot from his story and his journey to India. Without a vision, Jobs was lost. But if he had just come back with a vision, and didn't bother putting a plan into action, the story would have ended there, and we might not even know the name "Steve Jobs."

The ultimate lesson is this: while you can't reach the vision without a plan, the vision is the foundation that keeps you moving toward something special.

> *While you can't reach the vision without a plan, the vision is the foundation that keeps you moving toward something special.*

That's why the first step in the One of a Kind Financial Plan™ is and always will be discovering your vision for your one-of-a-kind life. That's why the first time I meet with clients, I ask them the kinds of questions I've encouraged you to ask yourself throughout this book, about what life experiences you want to have, what matters most to you, what type of life you would live if money wasn't a factor.

Sometimes it takes hours to draw those answers out—but I can't move forward without that foundation. I'm not a travel agent or a spiritual guide or a life coach. But as a financial planner, I've learned that the only plans worth making are the ones that start with your life, your dreams, and your priorities—your vision.

GETTING CLEAR ON YOUR VISION

Back in Chapter 3, I asked you to reflect on some questions to help you start imagining what your one-of-a-kind life might look like. Think back to the answers that came to mind:

1. *Why is money important to you?*

2. *What excites you every day?*

3. *What gets you out of bed in the morning?*

4. *What would you do if you knew you never had to worry about money?*

5. *What is something you're never late for because you genuinely want to be there?*

6. *What brings a smile to your face whenever you think about it?*

7. *What feels effortless and doesn't seem like work?*

8. *What do you hope your children, grandchildren, or friends will remember about you after you're gone?*

9. *Where would you escape to if you could go anywhere?*

10. *Where do you feel most at peace?*

11. *What could you happily do every day?*

It wasn't just an exercise to spark daydreams. It was the beginning of your One of a Kind Financial Plan™.

Now that you're ready to start putting your plan together, I'm going to ask you to dig deeper into the answers you uncovered with those questions.

Look back at your answers (and if you didn't take the time before to ask yourself these questions, do so now). Using those answers, visualize what your ideal life will look like one year from now. Then five years from now. Then ten. Then in retirement.

Where do you live? Who's with you? Who is important to you? What does your day-to-day look like? Where are you putting your time and energy? What keeps you going? How is your one-of-a-kind life evolving and changing through the seasons of life?

Here's the most important part—dream big. Don't censor yourself. Let yourself think beyond what you've been told is possible. You can live a one-of-a-kind life—but you have to give yourself permission to understand what you really want.

SO...HOW MUCH DO YOU NEED TO GET THERE?

Here's the part in this journey where you might expect me to walk you through some math to get to a certain number—the number that will make your one-of-a-kind life a reality. But as I covered in Chapter 7, it doesn't work that way.

Here's why. Let's imagine two completely separate, disconnected people—we'll call them Todd and Ingrid.

Let's say that they both love to travel. Maybe they even want to travel to the same places, the same number of times a year. And let's even pretend for the sake of argument that they are both 50 years old, earn a similar salary, and each has two children who are the same ages.

Even then, with all of those similarities, their One of a Kind Financial Plan™ still wouldn't look the same. They likely haven't saved the exact amount of money. They definitely aren't going to experience the same life situations or unexpected expenses. And their lives just aren't going to follow the exact same path.

Maybe Todd wants to travel while still working until he's 70. Maybe Ingrid wants to retire when she's 57 years old.

Maybe Todd's children have medical concerns that are going to require more of his focus and money. Maybe Ingrid wants to pay for her children's college or leave a trust for her grandchildren.

Maybe Todd wants to stay in big cities and visit museums and experience art when he travels, while Ingrid wants to take train rides around countries and see as many cities as possible.

Maybe Todd also wants to start a scholarship in his family's name. Maybe Ingrid wants to purchase land to pass down.

There are too many possibilities to even begin listing them all, but the point is this: "One of a kind" isn't a catchphrase. It's called that because it's true. Your life isn't like anyone else's, and your financial plan shouldn't be either.

The One of a Kind Financial Plan™ is about thinking differently. We're not chasing a number. We're solving for your unknowns by controlling what we can about your finances and building a fund for the rest. We're addressing your fears by creating income and establishing a long-term care plan. We're growing your money strategically with an investment strategy built with a purpose in mind. We're looking at *everything* involved and building a plan specifically for you.

As you look at your vision to start to build your plan, I do encourage you to start thinking about what your costs might look like to support where you want to live, what adventures you want to take, how you want to help people, and the legacy you want to leave behind.

But I also want you to remember that when you have a financial plan in place that accounts for all of it, one that addresses the what-ifs, that shows you that you're secure, that controls what you can control, and that is specifically created so that you can go live the life you want, it's much more powerful than chasing a number ever will be. Until you have those pieces in place, that number goal isn't going to do anything for you.

The greatest risk any of us faces is the uncertainty of the future. It could be a sudden health challenge, a geopolitical shift, or even another global crisis. The unknown is always there, and we can't control it.

What we *can* control is how we live today. No one else can live your life for you. If there are things you want to do, places you want to see, goals you want to achieve, or people you want to connect with—there's no better time to start than now.

In the next few chapters, I'm going to break down the other steps you can take to start creating your One of a Kind Financial Plan™, whether you're going to do it yourself, work with someone else, or come work with me.

CHAPTER 12

BUILD YOUR TEAM

I recently had a one-of-a-kind experience in Peru hiking Montaña Arcoíris, also known as Rainbow Mountain.

This magnificent mountain has become a magnet for outdoor enthusiasts and adventurers, and once you see pictures, it's easy to know why. The mountain overlooks a valley composed of colorful minerals, which creates a rainbow-colored landscape that can take your breath away.

And what's interesting about this is that up until about 15 years ago, it was covered in snow. It was a hidden gem we didn't even know about. Now, though, people come from all over the world to see it.

But it's not an easy place to get to—you have to take a four-hour bus ride from Cusco to get to the base of the mountain and a steep hike to the summit that lasts about an hour and a half. The elevation is about 16,500 feet (for reference, the Mount Everest Base Camp is 17,598).

When you start the hike, you can see a little bit of the landscape around you, but you can't get the real, breathtaking view of the valley unless you hike up to the mountaintop.

My wife and I started the hike with our tour guide, César. And pretty soon, I started to feel sick from the higher elevation. It was difficult to breathe. My stomach felt ill. And I started to think, "*There's no way I'm going to make it to the top.*"

I tried to push myself, but by the time we got a third of the way to the summit, I was ready to throw in the towel.

I told César and my wife, "I'm tapping out. I need to stop. You guys go ahead. I'm not going to make it."

César told me, "Okay, hey, just take five more steps."

I took five more steps.

He prompted me again, "Let's just take ten more."

I took the ten steps.

He pointed ahead and told me, "In the next ten minutes, we're going to be at that hut up there. Can you get there?"

He kept going like that, parceling out our progress up the mountain about ten more times, keeping me moving a few steps at a time.

Three times I told him, "This is it—-I can't go on any further." The air was thin, and I was breathing heavily trying to get enough oxygen into my lungs. Mentally, I thought I was done.

But he kept pushing me little by little.

The thing is, I'd traveled 99.9% of the distance I needed to reach the summit—from Norfolk, Virginia travelling all the way to Peru. Then came the long arduous bus ride to the base of the mountain. I'd started the entire journey a week before.

And now, I was less than a half hour from having an experience that most people won't ever have. And here, I wanted to quit. My mind swirled.

César had been with us all week. I had shared with him

a lot about my business, all about the one-of-a-kind life philosophy, about how much my wife and I love to travel and have these adventures together. He knew that this was an experience I wanted to have. And he knew how to keep me going—one step at a time.

Take five steps. Take ten steps. Make it to that hut. He prompted me at least a dozen times. And it was working!

When we were just ten steps from the top, he turned to me and joked, "Hey, you want to quit now? You're getting ready to see one of the most amazing sights you'll ever experience in your life."

When we finally reached the summit, I looked down at the view. And I sat there for 30 minutes, in silence, taking it in. The view was majestic—I've never seen anything like it. It was truly one of a kind.

I kept thinking, "Holy cow. I almost turned back. I almost quit. I almost didn't make it that last 0.1% of the journey to get here."

And if it wasn't for César, I wouldn't have. I would have turned back. I would have missed it.

That's the power of having a guide that keeps you moving—someone alongside you to keep you going, even when it would be easier to turn back.

And that's why once you build your vision and determine what it is you really want, the next step for your one-of-a-kind life is to find the guide who can create a plan to take you there and build the team to support you.

WHO'S GUIDING YOUR TEAM?

It's no surprise that I believe you need a financial planner on your team—the kind who's going to push you toward the vision you have built. You need a César: someone who isn't going to let you give up, who is going to push you toward experiences that change your life. You need a guide who knows what to do to help you reach your one-of-a-kind life.

And here's the thing—that person doesn't have to be me. Maybe I'm the right fit for you, maybe I'm not. Maybe you're ready to move forward with me, maybe you want to look at other options. There's nothing wrong with that.

What I do want is for you to make sure you have the right person—someone who isn't following the traditional path or just giving you the same financial plan they give everybody else.

So...how will you know if they're the right financial guide for you? If you're still here with me at this point, you're probably ready to do things differently when it comes to finances. And that means you need a financial planner who's going to do things differently as well.

Here are some red flags to watch out for, indicators that the person you're working with or considering working with is *not* going to be that one-of-a-kind guide for you:

- They provide the same solution for everybody (e.g., they only sell life insurance policies or, if you were referred to them by a friend, you are getting the same solution your friend got).
- They provide a solution but they don't tell you the reasons why.
- They only give you general talking points instead of thorough explanations.

- They only meet with you once a year, or not at all (I'll talk more about this shortly).
- They don't ask you about the life you want.
- They say, "Let's execute this one strategy and then we'll come back and do something else later" instead of creating a comprehensive plan.
- They are limited in what they can offer you.
- They won't tell you what they're invested in personally or show you their assets.

That last one might surprise you, but it's one of the easiest ways to gauge the person you're going to work with. Are they *really* offering you the best solution? Or are they toeing a company line or pushing a product, like I talked about in Chapter 5? Asking them to show you their assets and their returns on investments, is an easy litmus test.

If they can't or won't share with you what they're invested in, they are probably more interested in selling you a product than in giving you big-picture solutions. (For all you know, they're invested in plenty of other options than what they're offering for you.)

I believe in what I offer my clients. That's why I'll show my assets and investments to anyone who asks in their consultation.

I *want you* to question what I'm saying. I want you to know that I have your back. I want you to be able to trust that I'm helping you get to where you want to go.

And if you work with someone else, I want you to have that same trust level. So ask the questions. Push back. Make sure that the person you're bringing onto your financial team is going to create something specifically for you.

Ask them to show you their assets.

Ask them to explain why the solutions they're offering make sense for *you*.

Ask them what they're licensed to provide; and what they cannot provide.

Ask them about every step of the One of a Kind Financial Plan™ I unpacked in Chapter 9 (tax planning, retirement income, investment management, long-term care, and legacy planning).

And, if they work for a major firm, ask them what the company philosophy is and how often the firm deviates from it.

Don't shy away from these questions. You deserve to know that your financial planner is a supportive teammate for you.

ARE YOU BUILDING A RELATIONSHIP?

The other big question to ask yourself about your financial advisor is: are you building a relationship, or are you just a number to them?

> *How can someone who doesn't know you have your best interests at heart? How could they ever help you make decisions with your money?*

When you work with a big company, you might not even have a designated advisor. Even if you do, you might get moved around or have difficulty connecting with the person who is supposed to be handling your financial future. If you have a question, it's quite possible you're going to call a number, get put on hold, and still might not end up on the phone with someone who knows you or anything about you.

How could that possibly be fiduciary? How can someone who doesn't know you have your best interests at heart? How could they ever help you make the best decisions about your money, your retirement?

If you want a financial plan that's built specifically for you, you have to work with an advisor who has a relationship with you. That doesn't mean someone who entered numbers into a spreadsheet on your behalf or met with you one time to give you a presentation. It means someone who takes the time to know who you are right away, who's familiar with your dreams, your family, and your lifestyle. It means someone who is actively working to make sure that your plan is firing on all cylinders even when your life changes.

We connect with our clients regularly via email, social media, mail, or phone calls. We speak directly with our clients at least six times a year, checking in, asking questions, and continuing to build that relationship and trust with them so that we are able to offer real guidance and support.

And for our clients who want to reduce the number of emails received or hear from us less often, that's okay too. (A real relationship means we respect what works for *you*.)

But the bottom line is, we *know* you. We want to hear about the one-of-a-kind life you're living—the adventures, the experiences, the ups and downs. Then, when questions or financial concerns do come up, we're already up to date, and we can make sure that your plan keeps moving forward.

That's what a relationship with a One of a Kind Financial Planner looks like…and you shouldn't settle for anything less.

WHO ELSE IS ON YOUR TEAM?

On any great team, everybody has different roles. Let's say you're training to climb Mount Everest. You're going to need a Sherpa as your guide.

You'll also need others who help you reach your summit goal. You might work with a personal trainer on your fitness to get into shape. You might train with a mountaineering coach well before you arrive at the base camp. Maybe you bring in a travel agent to plan the trip.

But what if you had one point person, one guide, to bring the rest of your team members into the right places to solve the challenges you're facing?

That's what your financial planner should do. That might mean bringing in certain professionals, or it might mean providing tools or software in their place, depending on what your needs are. The teammates might include CPAs, insurance agents, long-term care providers, and attorneys. But instead of asking you to find these individuals on your own and then to maintain the team you build with no communication, we work to pull it all together for you. We drive the action to build an effective team that keeps you moving toward your vision.

Your team isn't just made up of professionals, though. It's also made up of the people close to you in your life—like my wife was part of my team heading to Rainbow Mountain.

One-of-a-kind financial planners will also bring these other team members to the table to help you when necessary.

Who is going to be your point of communication if you're unable to communicate with your team members? For example, who will make sure the decisions you want for long-term care are followed? Who in your family or circle is going to advocate for you? Those are the people we need to recruit on your team as well.

Your team is strongest when someone keeps everyone organized, drives action and communication, and makes sure everything is ready for the next play. That's one of the key jobs of a one-of-a-kind financial planner.

THE TEAM THAT SUPPORTS YOUR ONE-OF-A-KIND LIFE

Beyond the team that helps you create your One of a Kind Financial Plan™, you're also going to need to have people who help support your one-of-a-kind lifestyle.

That might mean a great travel agent or a fitness instructor. It might mean an expert on genealogy or rare historical items or whatever it might be that plays into making your dream life a reality.

And it absolutely should be the people who love and support you the most in your life—the ones who will cheer you on and encourage you to live a one-of-a-kind life.

THE TAKEAWAY

Just like I couldn't get to the top of Rainbow Mountain by myself, you can't achieve your one-of-a-kind life alone. You need a team that's going to support you every step of the way.

That team should include:

- A financial planner who creates a comprehensive, customized plan for you.
- Professionals (or software and tools) that help you execute your plan. (In the One of a Kind Financial Plan™, we bring these teammates in for you.)
- And the people who will support you and help you live your one-of-a-kind life.

Most importantly, the financial planner you choose needs to be someone who builds a relationship with you—someone who knows you, someone who communicates with you, someone who is there for you when questions or concerns come up or when life throws curveballs. It is someone you can truly trust to care about your financial future.

CHAPTER 13

BUILD YOUR KNOWLEDGE

We live in a fast-paced world that has us always on the go, needing to work more, do more, and cram more productivity into our day.

So if you haven't built a foundation of financial knowledge for yourself, it's easy to understand the reason why. It's tempting to put financial planning off altogether, thinking you'll get around to it later. It's comforting to think that somebody else will take care of building this knowledge for you so you can just forget about doing the work.

But financial planning isn't like car insurance—you don't just make a few decisions, send a check, forget about it, and hope that you're covered if something goes wrong. You *will* need the results of your financial plan. You can't just be a passive participant in your financial future.

How will you know that the life you want to live is attainable? How will you be sure that you have enough to live comfortably in retirement? How will you know what you're able to do *now* with your money while still staying on track for your future?

How will you know that your numbers add up? That you can trust the people you have handling your money currently?

It's unfortunate to say, but an ignorant person is the easiest to con—and not everyone out there *is* trustworthy.

You're the one who's going to have to live with your financial outcome. It's your future at stake. So why would you ever settle for a financial plan that keeps you in the dark?

You don't need a degree in finance or to spend months reading investment theories and economic books. But you do owe it to yourself to build a basic level of financial knowledge that informs you about what's happening with your money.

WHAT SHOULD YOU KNOW?

I've mentioned throughout this book that the One of a Kind Financial Plan™ involves financial education so that you can be an active participant. A big part of what I do is finding ways to simplify the topics you need to understand so that you can gain the right education without feeling lost or overwhelmed.

But this isn't just something I want to offer to my clients. I want *everyone* out there to have access to the financial knowledge they need to build the life they want, whether they build a One of a Kind Financial Plan™ with me or not.

Here are some of the things I believe you need to get familiar with (don't worry if you aren't knowledgeable on these topics yet—I'll point you to some free resources that can help):

- What tax strategies are right for you in your situation to reduce taxes now and in the future
- Should you start a business as a tax strategy
- What types of retirement accounts are available, and which ones involve tax-free withdrawals
- How much money you can contribute to different types of accounts
- How to create a budget to track income and expenses
- How to determine how much money you should be saving
- How much of an emergency fund you should save
- Types of assets that can create retirement income
- What are RMD (Required Minimum Distributions) and why do you have to take them
- Should you have a ROTH IRA or a Backdoor ROTH IRA
- How stocks are bought, sold, and traded
- The difference between stocks, ETFs, and mutual funds
- What types of investments are "safer" and what types are "riskier"
- The pros and cons of annuities
- How much money you'll need to support your long-term care wishes
- What types of long-term care insurance policies are available
- What components go into writing a will
- What types of trusts you can create
- How to avoid probate

- What you should really leave to your family as a legacy

I've talked about some of these pieces throughout the book—and you can find many of these terms in the glossary at the back of this book for more details. Unfortunately, if I tried to cover everything on the list, what I have shared in detail, not only would this book be way too long and potentially overwhelming for you, but I would also run the risk of giving you outdated information if changes happen in the government, the tax code, or any part of the financial world. The financial industry *does* change and evolve.

That's why I've created free online resources for you on my website and YouTube channel, where you can find consistently updated educational videos that break down even the most complex financial planning topics in simple ways, along with our interactive learning platform. (I've included those links in the resources section at the end of this book for you as a thank you for joining me on this journey and reading along.)

BE AN ACTIVE PARTICIPANT IN YOUR FUTURE

Remember, you're the one who is going to live with the choices you make in your financial plan. And that means that you need to be actively involved.

By all means, bring in the experts. Let someone with experience and knowledge help you make decisions and guide you through all of the steps involved. But don't do it blindly. Build the knowledge you need first to protect yourself, your money, and your future.

Financial podcaster and author Dave Ramsey often says that a common characteristic of wealthy individuals is "they pay attention."[12] I believe that to live a one-of-a-kind life you have to:

- Have a vision for that life (see Chapter 11)
- Give that vision your full attention
- And build the right team—a team you trust—to help you accomplish that vision.

12 Ramsey, Dave. *The Ramsey Show*. Ramsey Solutions. https://www.ramseysolutions.com/shows/the-ramsey-show.

CHAPTER 14

BUILD YOUR ROADMAP

Once you have the vision, team, and your financial knowledge in place, you can start solving the challenges you face and putting pieces into play to make your vision a reality.

The One of a Kind Financial Plan™ is that roadmap. It solves the problems that prevent your vision from becoming a reality, so you can pay attention to what matters most: living your one-of-a-kind life.

For some, that plan means saving a little bit more money. For others, it means shifting from saving to investing so you allow your money to do the work for you. And for some, it's strategically converting accounts to reduce taxes now.

Just like I can't give you a specific number to reach for the retirement you desire, I also can't give you a specific path to achieve that goal. There are plenty of people who will try to tell you there is one surefire path to a "successful" retirement—but those people aren't advisors who will create a One of a Kind Financial Plan™.

The truth is that financial planning is like redecorating your home. Some people just need to reorganize and move furniture around to get the look they want. Others need to declutter, let go of things. Others need a complete redesign, tearing everything down and starting from scratch.

You might be in a great place having completed some of the steps in the One of a Kind Financial Plan™. Maybe your investments are solid, and you just need some tweaking on your retirement income or your legacy planning.

Maybe you need to keep doing exactly what you're doing right now and you now need a long-term care plan in place.

Maybe, like most of the people who contact me, you've saved money but you've never touched any of the steps needed in a comprehensive financial plan that brings everything together.

Maybe you've never done any planning and haven't saved enough—and it's time to really get moving on the road to your financial future, starting with tax planning and then building to the rest of the steps I covered in Chapter 9.

Whatever it is, the financial plan has to be created specifically to get YOU from where YOU are now to where YOU want to be—and that doesn't happen by accident.

THE FIRST STEP TO BUILDING YOUR ONE OF A KIND FINANCIAL PLAN™

So…how do you get from Point A to Point B? How do you create your One of a Kind Financial Plan™, let alone your one-of-a-kind life? Like most big challenges in life, it starts with one simple step.

There are many universal truths in the world passed down from generation to generation.

Finish these for me:

- Where there is a will, there is a _____. — George Herbert
- The only way to eat an elephant is _____. —Desmond Tutu
- The best time to plant an apple tree was_____. And the second best time is _____. —Chinese proverb
- A journey of a thousand miles begins with _____. —Lao Tzu

Answers:

- Where there is a will, there is a **way**.
- The only way to eat an elephant is **one bite at a time.**
- The best time to plant an apple tree was **20 years ago**. And the second best time is **now**.
- A journey of a thousand miles begins **with a single step.**

What do these all have in common? They focus on an outcome, and, more importantly, where to *start* to make that outcome a reality—and that is by taking action.

So, for a custom-designed financial plan, what's that starting point? Organization. Think back to Chapter 4 where I talked about the barriers that most people face when it comes to financial planning. Disorganization is one of the biggest barriers.

If you have the digital equivalent of a shoebox full of envelopes, receipts, accounts, and assets, it's time to start sorting it.

A good financial planner can help you with the heavy lifting, but if you want to start the ball rolling more efficiently, take some time to educate yourself on the following:

- Where your accounts are located
- How to log into them
- How much money is where
- What your expenses are
- How much debt you have, if any
- What you're invested in currently
- What your company match is on your retirement plan

Once you get that information organized, you can start to create your roadmap. To help you get started, I have a tool that can map out your assets to create a balance sheet and help you see where you're headed currently.

This isn't a magic button—but it is a great tool to help you start getting organized and begin thinking about your finances comprehensively. (See the resources section at the end of this book for a link to fill out your roadmap.)

DON'T MISS OUT ON YOUR ONE-OF-A-KIND LIFE

W e've reached the end of our journey in these pages. I hope you've learned something new—not only the ins and outs of the financial industry and tax planning and retirement income and what a "legacy" really means (although those are undoubtedly important topics).

But what I hope you have learned most of all is how to think differently about your financial plan, about your life, and about what money can mean for you.

(And if you are a financial advisor or an aspiring one, I hope that reading this book has shown you that there is more to the industry than selling products. You can choose to serve your clients differently, empowering them in their lives and making a real impact. If this book resonated with you, reach out—we're always looking for new one-of-a-kind financial planners to join our team!)

To recap everything we've learned so far:

- I covered why I believe that financial planning should be a path to create a one-of-a-kind life: the life you would live if money weren't a factor. I shared my personal story, and the story of my brother, who lived a truly unique, truly full life in the 41 years he had on this earth.

- I talked about why the traditional financial industry, which focuses on number goals and saving without a purpose and cookie-cutter rules, doesn't equip you with what you need to live and retire the way you want.

- I walked you through how to visualize your one-of-a-kind life, including your Retirement CHI™ (community, health, and impact).

- I covered the barriers that keep people from living a one-of-a-kind life and the barriers that keep them from creating a One of a Kind Financial Plan™.

- I discussed the problems in the financial industry, from the Piecemeal Effect to the problems with finding true fiduciaries, to interpreting the minefield of advice.

- I explained why tax planning is the one thing you can do to make the biggest impact on your financial future, and why it's the cornerstone of the One of a Kind Financial Plan™.

- I walked you through the five steps involved in a One of a Kind Financial Plan™ (tax planning, retirement income, investment management, long-term care planning, and legacy planning).

- And I explained how to build your vision, build your team, build your knowledge, and build your roadmap.

- I also shared several stories of clients near and dear to my heart. Each story brings in a lifetime of unique experiences—and each story shows the true value of living a one-of-a-kind life.

MOVING FORWARD

You have three options from here:

Option 1: The Traditional Path

You can choose to work with a traditional financial advisor, taking your accounts and statements in and showing them what you have. They'll tell you, "Here's where you are, and here's the number you can get to."

They'll decide where you're going. They'll tell *you* what kind of life is possible for you.

The traditional path turns financial planning into an assembly line. Everyone gets the same thing, and they can get better and faster at selling it.

That doesn't mean you'll lose all of your money or throw away your financial future. They're not out to rob you. You can live a "good" life by going down this route. But the question to ask yourself is…do you want what they have to offer you? Do you want to chase a number? Or do you want to decide the experiences that you want and build a plan that helps you get there?

Option 2: The DIY Path

Can you go it alone? Sure, it's possible. The tools in the One of a Kind Financial Plan™ aren't unheard of. You can learn about them, make your own choices, and build your plan yourself. If you have the time, tools, and knowledge, and you understand the intricacies of your financial choices and how they work together comprehensively, go for it.

I'll even help you get started—use the resources at the end of this book to your advantage. And if you decide it's too much, you can reach out to book a call anytime.

Option 3: The Customized Path

Your financial plan shouldn't be factory-made. That's why the One of a Kind Financial Plan™ exists—to break away from the cookie-cutter mold—and to design something that's truly yours.

Your life deserves more than one-size-fits-all advice.

From here, you get to decide where you go. If you want to work with me, my team and I are ready. If you want to learn more about us, please reach out. If you want to focus on building your knowledge, use my resources and learn everything you can.

But whatever you choose to do, I hope that you remember the stories I've shared—especially my brother Jonathan. Without him, and the reminder of how quickly everything can change—I wouldn't have realized how important it is to fully embrace life and live the unique one that makes you happy.

We aren't guaranteed anything in the future...which is why you deserve to live the life you want, now and every day.

If you're ready to make it happen, I'd be happy to be on your team. Book a call to get started—let's start the journey to your one-of-a-kind life!

Head to mikemilligan.com!

Cheering you on,

Mike

The One of a Kind Financial Plan™ For Your One of a Kind Life!

GLOSSARY

Annuity: A financial contract offered by life insurance companies that offers benefits to meet your financial needs.

Assets Under Management: A financial advising model where advisors charge a percentage fee based on the total amount of investments they manage for you.

Assets Under Contract: A financial advising model where advisors are paid commission based on selling a product.

Assets Under Influence: A financial advising model where advisors influence your strategy without directly managing your investments. You're paying for their expertise, not specific actions they take with your money.

Backdoor Roth IRA: A strategy to contribute to a Roth IRA indirectly to bypass the income limits for direct Roth IRA contributions, by making a non-deductible contribution to a traditional IRA and then converting that IRA to a Roth IRA.

Balance Sheet: A financial statement that shows your assets, your liabilities, and your net worth.

Bonds: Fixed-income investments where you lend money to an entity, like a government or corporation, in exchange for regular interest payments and the return of the principal amount at a set date.

Certificates of Deposit (CDs): A savings account with a fixed interest rate and maturity date. You agree to leave your money in the account for a set term, and in return, the bank may pay you higher interest than a regular savings account. However, withdrawing early may result in penalties.

Employee Retirement Income Security Act (ERISA): A federal law that sets minimum standards for most voluntarily established retirement and health plans in private industry to protect individuals in these plans. Enacted in response to concerns about mismanagement and abuse of private pension funds, ERISA aims to safeguard the interests of employee benefit plan participants and their beneficiaries.

Financial literacy: The ability to use financial understanding to make informed decisions about your money.

Fiduciary: Someone legally obligated to act in your "best interest."

Guaranteed retirement income (also known as fixed income): Retirement funds that are designated, fixed, and not dependent on the stock market.

Indexed Universal Life (IUL): A life insurance policy with a death benefit, living benefits, and the potential for cash value growth based on the indexes in the contract.

Pension plans: Employer-funded accounts that pay out monthly in retirement.

Probate: The legal process of overseeing the distribution of a deceased person's assets according to their will, or according to state law if there is no will.

Retirement income: Money you have to support yourself in retirement, either received through Social Security or a pension or withdrawn from retirement accounts such as 401(k)s or IRAs.

Required Minimum Distribution (RMD): Minimum amounts individuals must withdraw annually from certain retirement accounts, like traditional IRAs or 401(k)s, starting at a specific age, as mandated by the IRS. These withdrawals are taxed as income.

Roth IRA: A type of individual retirement account (IRA) where you contribute after-tax dollars, eliminating taxes on your future earnings and qualified withdrawals.

Securities and Exchange Commission (SEC): The United States government agency in charge of monitoring the financial markets and protecting investors.

Trust: A legal arrangement in which a person or entity (the grantor) transfers assets to a trustee, who manages them for the benefit of one or more beneficiaries according to the terms outlined in a trust agreement. Trusts can be used for estate planning, asset protection, tax benefits, and charitable giving.

Variable retirement income: Retirement funds that can fluctuate with the stock market.

401(k): An employer-sponsored retirement savings plan that allows employees to contribute a portion of their wages, often before taxes, to individual retirement accounts.

RESOURCES

For retirees and future retirees:

- To read white papers and access our interactive learning platform, head to www.mikemilligan.com.
- For consistently updated videos on every step of the One of a Kind Financial Plan™ and everything you need to know about your finances, visit my YouTube Channel.
- For more financial literacy, listen to my podcast, Ideas by Mike.
- Fill out your roadmap and start to see where your plan can take you at www.mikemilligan.com/roadmap.
- For more information about CFP® professionals, visit https://www.letsmakeaplan.org/.

For financial professionals:

- For information about becoming a CFP®, visit https://www.cfp.net/.
- For support with launching your own book, visit https://www.peacefulprofits.com/.
- For more information about joining our nationwide team, visit www.mikemilligan.com.

ABOUT THE AUTHOR

Mike Milligan is an independent financial advisor and creator of the One of a Kind Financial Plan™. He has received his CFP® (CERTIFIED FINANCIAL PLANNER™) and Accredited Investment Fiduciary® (AIF®) designations.

With 25 years of experience in the financial industry, Mike has seen firsthand how many people fall through the cracks with a traditional advising approach. He has dedicated himself and his firm to teaching people that there is a different, better way to approach financial planning—one that creates customized plans to support clients to live their ideal lives.

Mike also serves as an adjunct lecturer at Old Dominion University, teaching future financial professionals about the principles and ethics of financial planning.

When he isn't helping clients reach their one-of-a-kind lives, he's traveling with his wife Leigh Ana or spending time with his children, grandchildren, and his two dogs.

Mike believes that everyone deserves to live their ideal life—one filled with experiences, adventures, and purpose.

www.ingramcontent.com/pod-product-compliance
Lightning Source LLC
Chambersburg PA
CBHW071234210326
41597CB00016B/2045